AF361587

MEAT
MATTERS

SEPHARDI AND MIZRAHI STUDIES

Harvey E. Goldberg and Matthias Lehmann, editors

MEAT MATTERS

ETHNOGRAPHIC REFRACTIONS OF THE BETA ISRAEL

HAGAR SALAMON

INDIANA UNIVERSITY PRESS

This book is a publication of

Indiana University Press
Office of Scholarly Publishing
Herman B Wells Library 350
1320 East 10th Street
Bloomington, Indiana 47405 USA

iupress.org

Manufactured in the United States of America

First printing 2023

Library of Congress Cataloging-in-Publication Data

Names: Salamon, Hagar, author.
Title: Meat matters : ethnographic refractions of the Beta Israel / Hagar Salamon.
Description: Bloomington : Indiana University Press, [2023] | Series: Sephardi and Mizrahi studies | Includes bibliographical references and index.
Identifiers: LCCN 2022057544 (print) | LCCN 2022057545 (ebook) | ISBN 9780253065773 (hardback) | ISBN 9780253065780 (paperback) | ISBN 9780253065803 (ebook)
Subjects: LCSH: Jews, Ethiopian—Israel—Social life and customs. | Jews, Ethiopian—Israel—Rites and ceremonies. | Livestock—Israel. | Meat—Israel. | BISAC: HISTORY / Middle East / Israel & Palestine | SOCIAL SCIENCE / Jewish Studies
Classification: LCC DS113.8.F34 S25 2023 (print) | LCC DS113.8.F34 (ebook) | DDC 305.892/405694—dc23/eng/20230111
LC record available at https://lccn.loc.gov/2022057544
LC ebook record available at https://lccn.loc.gov/2022057545

CONTENTS

PREFACE

Sometimes it takes years to see what you are looking at. I have been studying the Ethiopian Jews and their expressive culture for over thirty years. Only recently have I come to realize the unique significance of issues that emerged in our very first encounters. Soon after the first major wave of Ethiopian Jews arrived in Israel, still living in absorption centers, I witnessed animated discussions revolving around the purchase, slaughter, and taste of sheep and cattle in Israel. The newcomers had survived a long, painful trek from their villages in Ethiopia followed by a prolonged, devastating sojourn in Sudan. On arrival, they faced a shockingly unfamiliar setting totally foreign to their previous way of life.

The bewilderment and confusion that prevailed in this period were obvious. Still, despite all the chaos and as if out of nowhere, animals, with their essential concreteness, dominated conversations. I noted the sheer excitement that accompanied these discussions but at the time did not appreciate its wide-ranging significance. The newly arrived immigrants kept referring to both livestock and fresh meat. Unlike my new friends but similarly to most of my contemporaries, I had no wish to connect the steak to the cow. I avoided the gory details and recoiled from any tangible image of the overall implied scene. I had no familiarity with butchering and no special interest in the procedures involved. Nevertheless, in the many yet-to-come in-depth interviews on which this book is based, meat-related topics repeatedly emerged.

Throughout the years, interviews were held mainly in Hebrew and occasionally in Amharic or Tigrinya (with the help of younger, bilingual family members). Although they were about issues utterly foreign to our shared present reality, these conversations were based on the implied assumption of the translatability of the topics. Throughout these conversations, however, I was struck by a number of cultural terms that defied translation. Hebrew wordings ceased to suffice. My interlocutors would reach a momentary impasse. No Hebrew terms could convey some of the most intimate parts of their prior life. But their determination to convey and share these culturally specific ideas was clearly relentless. Such moments turned out to be priceless to our dialogue. They were points of entry, cracks that allowed us to probe together into cultural subtleties that otherwise would likely never have arisen in our discussions. One example of such an impasse revolved around *kircha*.[1] Over the years I was deluged with vivid accounts of the prices of sheep before Passover, advice for the best places to purchase live cattle, and incessant invitations to participate in a kircha. The ample ethnographic details surrounding kircha illuminate a highly particularistic Ethiopian term, whose full significance only gradually emerged (as did its pertinence to the issues of this book). Therefore, at this launching point, I invite the reader to a brief account of the journey undertaken to decipher this deeply rooted cultural modality and to trace its transformation from the Ethiopian context to that of Israel.

A kircha, as I eventually learned, is a group established for the purpose of purchasing, slaughtering, and dividing meat among friends and family members. Gradually my curiosity was aroused. I heard the details of the butchery, the strict means of division of the animal's body into small and equal chunks, and the concluding lottery ritual for the distribution of the meat among the participants. But I still was reluctant to witness the actual spectacle.

It was during a visit to rural Ethiopia many years later that I got to see a kircha firsthand. By pure chance I found myself in the midst of a group of local men facing a decapitated ox. Its whole body had just been chopped up into small pieces and, in front of my eyes, was being reorganized into a few dozen identical meat piles, over which a lottery was subsequently performed. Confronted with their overt enthusiasm, I finally grasped, mentally and sensually, the irrepressible allure of the kircha.

Returning home, I was now eager to witness a kircha as performed in Israel. I entreated my friend, an Israeli Ethiopian certified by the rabbinate *shochet* (ritual slaughterer), to let me join him the next time he performed the entire procedure for a "meat group." It didn't take long before he invited me to participate in a kircha he was organizing. What I witnessed there sparked the writing of the present book.

This multilayered episode inspired a reexamination of the research itinerary I had followed throughout the years. What emerged more clearly than ever before was the presence of an overriding theme with elaborate variations. In countless stories as well as in numerous rituals, communal and familial, I had repeatedly come across descriptions of livestock, slaughter, and meat eating. They all pointed to the preeminence of meat matters and to a seemingly endless web of life-touching meanings. But it went even beyond that. Meat, with its multiplicity of references in food and ritual, is connected with other areas of experience. In the case of the Ethiopian Jews, meat is intrinsically involved with their own, visibly different bodies in Israel. Their bodies have become ever more pertinent in their negotiations of identity vis-à-vis other Jewish Israelis, and vis-à-vis religious authorities in particular.

It took all of my separate ethnographic studies on the Ethiopian Jews not only to identify the widespread prevalence of meat themes but also to confront the totality of their significance. Hence, through an exploration of the kircha, a revival of concrete ethnographic moments, and a reexamination of materials accumulated in a series of separate research projects, it became increasingly clear that meat matters are an ongoing and powerful focus of meaning in multiple realms of Ethiopian community life.[2] They continue to serve as key idioms, located at the heart of the conceptual and narrated processing of the dramatic transformation related to the move of Jews from Ethiopia to Israel. The present book is thus the outcome of a cumulative, contemplative process after years of ever-expanding ethnographic forays within a rapidly changing reality.[3]

Notes

1. Amharic terms will first appear in italics and thereafter in regular print. The transcription follows the system used by Leslau in his Concise Amharic-English Dictionary (1976). The linguistic root k-r-t (ch) of the term kircha and some of its related derivatives refer to the equal division of an object, of costs, or of obligations. For qərča (kircha), see Pankhurst (1988, 178), Kifleyesus (2003), Weber (2005), as well as Seleshe, Jo, and Lee (2014).

2. The polysemic quality of cattle, serving as icons of a traditional order and as tools in gaining control over modern life, was persuasively shown by Comaroff and Comaroff in relation to nineteenth-century Tswana (1990). On key symbols, see Ortner (1973) and Wagner (1986). On blood and body symbolism in general "in service to social intentions," see Douglas (1966).

3. Short sections of chapters 2 and 3 previously appeared in "Cow Tales: Decoding Images of Slavery in the Ethiopian Jewish Community," *Slavery & Abolition* 29, no. 3 (2008): 415–35. Short sections of chapter 4 appeared previously in *The Hyena People: Ethiopian Jews in Christian Ethiopia* (Berkeley: University of California Press, 1999). Sections of chapter 5 appeared previously in "Holy Meat, Black Slaughter: Power, Religion, Kosher Meat, and the Ethiopian-Israeli Community,"

in *Political Meals*, edited by Regina F. Bendix and Michaela Fenske, 273–85 (Munster: Wissenchaftsforum Kulinaristik, LIT, 2014); and in "Cutting into the Flesh of the Community: Ritual Slaughter, Meat Consumption, and the Transition from Ethiopia to Israel," *Studies in Contemporary Jewry 28* (2015): 110–45. Sections of chapter 6 previously appeared in "Misplaced Home and Mislaid Meat: Stories Circulating among Ethiopian Immigrants in Israel," *Callaloo* 33, no. 1 (2010): 165–76; and in "The Floor Falling Away: Dislocated Space and Body in the Humour of Ethiopian Immigrants in Israel," *Folklore* 122, no. 1 (2011): 16–34. Short sections of chapter 7 previously appeared in "Meat Lottery: A Spectacle in Transition from Ethiopia to Israel," *African and Black Diaspora* 11, no. 2 (2017): 129–43.

ACKNOWLEDGMENTS

This book is the result of a gradual coalescence of initially distinct research pathways carried out over the course of almost thirty years. I was interested in a wide range of topics related to Ethiopian Jews in Ethiopia and Israel and sought out their stories and insights. One research project led to the next, sometimes in unexpected ways. I followed each pathway, pursuing its central subject matter. In their stories, my interlocutors often provided answers well before I had formulated the questions. Engaged in research and writing on well-delineated themes, I was long unaware that behind the screen, so to speak, a book on meat matters was simultaneously being written.

It is due to this unintended accumulation of widely scattered revelations spanning time and space that the number of Ethiopian Israelis contributing to this book is vast. Their willingness to open their hearts and share their fond as well as painful memories, thoughts, and sentiments is greatly appreciated. Hopefully, this book to some extent reciprocates their generosity and trust.

Among the scores of interviewees spoken with throughout the years, I was fortunate to be assisted and befriended by a number of exceptional figures. I am indebted to the wealth of knowledge imparted to me by the late Dejen "Gideon" Mengesha and qes Avraham Tezazu. The ongoing friendships with Dejen's grandson, HaRav (Rabbi) Dr. Sharon Shalom, and with Yaffa Tezazu, qes Avraham's widow, help in sustaining a sense of vital connection with them. My gratitude is dispensed in full measure to HaRav (Rabbi) Yitshak Zegeye, who patiently shared his detailed memories and stimulating insights. Avraham "Abera" Pardo feted me with his painted animals, revealing deeply held sentiments that are beyond words.

Some of the matters central to this book, especially those related to slavery, were shared with me by people marked by dignity, honesty, and courage. In particular I wish to thank the people I have called Terengo, Habtesh, Radai, Almaz, and Mammit. I hope that their courageous voices will generate new and liberating understandings.

The emergence of meat matters from behind the screen led to the present book. In various stages of the writing of this book, I was fortunate to be encouraged and assisted by numerous people and institutions. Regina Bendix, Anbessa Teferra, and Ato Ayalew Mitiku provided intellectual stimulation and assistance. I am deeply grateful to Harvey Goldberg and Steven Kaplan for their wise and thoughtful comments on earlier drafts and for their enduring friendship. The advice provided by Chaim Rosen in regard to the final shaping of the book, as well as his generous sharing of knowledge and experience, are greatly appreciated. Galit Hasan-Rokem accompanied the book from its inception. Her insightful suggestions, abiding enthusiasm, and above all her sense of the human and moral dimensions of ethnographic research are a constant source of inspiration. I deeply thank Dan Levene, a fellow scholar and marvelous artist, for his generous contribution to the book. His talent, combined with an intimate familiarity with Ethiopian culture, are apparent in the painting that adorns the cover as well as the graphic design scattered throughout the book. I thank the anonymous referees of the book who offered, each from a different viewpoint, excellent suggestions contributing significantly to its final shape.

Thanks are owed to the fine institutions that supported the writing of this book: the Harry S. Truman Research Institute for the Advancement of Peace and Misgav Yerushalayim Research Center for the Heritage of Sephardi Jewry, both at the Hebrew University of Jerusalem. My gratitude is extended to the administrative staff as well as members of the Africa Unit of the Truman Institute for the outstanding collegial and supportive academic environment.

My family is a constant source of unfailing support. To Amos, my life partner, who gradually got caught up in the research project as a fieldwork companion and sensitive photographer, I wish to express my boundless appreciation and love. Our four daughters, Mika, Noga, Zohar, and Netta, each with her unique trajectory in life, provide the core of the entire enterprise.

MEAT MATTERS

Introduction

Life as lived and recounted by Ethiopian Jews has long fascinated me. For more than thirty years, I have been listening to stories that wander between Ethiopia and Israel in an attempt to explore personal and collective experiences. Ongoing conversations and in-depth interviews with people born in rural Ethiopia who moved to a new life in urban Israel are replete with a wealth of memories and tales related to the past, the present, and the interrelation between the two. In these manifold testimonies, one can discern ever-changing depictions of the dramatic move from homeland to Promised Land.

Known as Falasha or Beta Israel,[1] the Ethiopian Jews lived as a religious minority in the Horn of Africa until the last decades of the twentieth century. The exotic character of their identity as Black and Jewish has long captured the imagination of the Jewish world and of Christian missionaries and European explorers. While there are limited sources on the premodern history of the group, a significant body of literature on the Black Jews of Ethiopia emerged from the middle of the nineteenth century onward. A noteworthy portion of this literature speculates about their origins.

Dominant among these origin stories is the captivating Ethiopian legend of the meeting between King Solomon and the Queen of Sheba.[2] The Ethiopian version relays a deceitful seduction of the visiting queen by her host, resulting in a son named Menelik. As an adult, Menelik is believed to have traveled to Ethiopia from Jerusalem, accompanied by an Israelite entourage, taking with him the original Ark of the Covenant. In other narratives, various optional routes by which Israelites may have reached Ethiopia are suggested. In the late Middle Ages, the narrative of the "lost Tribe of Dan" became popular among Jews and gained prominence in the eyes of the religious authorities in Israel.[3]

Ethiopian Jews have been variously depicted as either an ancient Jewish group (a lost tribe in exile) or as an indigenous Ethiopian group.[4] The prevalence of the lost tribe conception had a formative and significant impact on this entire community. Each of these perspectives has been considered by people of different persuasions, and none has managed to prevail over the others. Without delving into the intrinsic interests of each, these specific speculations regarding origins capture attention for other reasons: primarily, they are able to mobilize wide-ranging data that play a constitutive role in matters regarding the lives of the Ethiopian Jews today, the central concern of my ethnographic approach.

Prior to their immigration (*Aliyah*, lit. "going up") to Israel, which began in the late 1970s, the Ethiopian Jews lived in small villages scattered across the vast highlands of rural northwestern Ethiopia, predominantly in the regions of Gondar (Bagemdar), Tigray, Walqayit, and Qwara. They were for the most part agriculturists, as well as smiths (men) and potters (women). Although a well-defined religious and occupational minority, they shared with their non-Jewish neighbors physical appearance as well as language. In Amharic-speaking areas the Beta Israel spoke Amharic, and in Tigrinya-speaking areas they spoke Tigrinya. Thus there was no unifying "Jewish" language in Ethiopia to set the Beta Israel apart (in writing or in speaking). Holy scriptures—for the Beta Israel the Old Testament (*Orit*) and for the Christians both the Old and the New Testaments—were written in *Ge'ez*, the ancient Ethiopian liturgical language used by both Christians and Jews for prayer and sacred writings. As a result, the Beta Israel shared an attachment to a biblical past with the dominant Christian population surrounding them. Indeed, Ethiopian Orthodox Christianity, the largest church among the Oriental Orthodox Christian churches, is unique in its Hebrew biblical orientation.[5] This context is, of course, significantly different from other Christian settings in which Jewish communities are found. One telling example connected with "marking the Jewish flesh" is that of male circumcision: in Ethiopia, both Jews and Christians performed the ritual on the eighth day, according to the biblical commandment. Thus, male circumcision was not considered a marker for Jewish identity. However, on arrival in Jewish Israel, the Beta Israel newcomers were obliged by the Chief Rabbinate to undergo a symbolic circumcision (a demand that was later revised, after raging demonstrations) in order to validate their Jewishness. Under the changing lens of meat-related issues, features of this fleshy mark will appear and reappear in different guises.

Despite the numerous similarities shared with their Christian neighbors, the Beta Israel perceived themselves as a separate religious group that steadfastly observed Judaism long after the majority of the Ethiopian population, as they believed, had forsaken it and shifted to the younger, soon-dominant Orthodox Christianity. The Orit, the central text of their faith, was used as the explicit basis for Ethiopian Jewish life and inspired their deeply ingrained dream of reaching Jerusalem. One of the distinguishing traits of the Beta Israel's religious traditions was the priests' (*qessotch*) nonhereditary status. Rather, priesthood was based, as it was for their Christian counterparts, on lengthy, specialized education. This practice was in marked contrast to the hereditary status of *kohanim* in rabbinic Judaism, and the implications of this distinction for sacrificial practices and ritual slaughter will be demonstrated throughout the book. Notably, the wide variety of Jewish cultures, represented here by the distinct Ethiopian Jewish traditions, facilitates a general appreciation of the richness of Jewish cultures that have emerged in encounters with different religious and cultural interfaces and specific dynamics of change.[6]

The enduring dream of reaching Jerusalem remained unfulfilled even following the founding of the State of Israel in 1948, when the mass immigration of many other far-flung Jewish communities was being encouraged. Despite their self-definition and struggles in Ethiopia as Jews, the Beta Israel were not immediately recognized as such under Israel's Law of Return.[7] Only in 1973, by means of an authoritative religious ruling based on a rabbinical opinion formulated more than four hundred years earlier,[8] were they officially recognized as Jews. Rabbi Ovadia Yosef, the then-incumbent Sephardi Chief Rabbi of Israel, declared that the Ethiopian Beta Israel community was descended from the lost Tribe of Dan.[9] In the wake of this definitive rabbinical ruling, it became possible to inaugurate the complex procedures required to enable the community's immigration to Israel.

Over the next nearly four decades, the bulk of the Beta Israel left Ethiopia for Israel in waves, the two largest and most dramatic of which were Operation Moses in 1984–85 and Operation Solomon in 1991.[10] In the subsequent quarter of a century, there was a continuous trickle of Beta Israel people found eligible for immigration to Israel. There has also emerged an ever-increasing inflow of Felasmura people (known also as Feres Mura in Ethiopia and Falashmura in Israel), descendants of Beta Israel who converted to Christianity in the past and have sought to return to Judaism by means of a specially designed conversion program,[11] who have emerged as the largest group among Israeli Ethiopians over the years. When the more than 45,000 children born in Israel are included, the Israeli Ethiopian community had by 2019 reached over 150,000. Their life in Israel, however, has been accompanied by a variety of persistent uncertainties regarding their Jewish identity, which have had divisive effects on both the community and larger Israeli society. Shadows of these issues will flicker throughout this book, often appearing in unanticipated, surprising contexts.

In presenting my findings to the reader, I seek to retain the enchantment of my visual, dialogic, and sensual experiences by producing a refracted text. Though decades have passed since the first groups of Beta Israel achieved their centuries-old dream of reaching Jerusalem, many individuals still harbor deep feelings of longing for what they left behind. After years of taking in a plethora of stories, it dawned on me that so much of what they said and described referred to livestock and meat. As they spoke I was transfixed by a powerful yearning, an almost physical ache that the people I listened to sustained for the animals—particularly the cows—they had abandoned on departing for Israel. These animals were depicted as organically connected to both the individual Ethiopian family and the group. Memories were indicative of strong emotions and an enduring commitment to the animals' well-being.

At the forefront of the Beta Israel's longing stand, so to speak, their beloved cows. What undeniably stays with Ethiopian immigrants, both as an idea and a symbol, is what their cows provided them: an array of functions, products, and sentiments of which meat was ultimate. Its significance as a meaningful mental and emotional currency remains crucial for deciphering a wide range of experiences. These ideas, so deeply rooted and compelling to the Beta Israel, generate activities and attitudes utterly foreign to their Israeli neighbors. Hopefully, this book will contribute to new understandings of these formerly insufficiently appreciated practices and beliefs.

For the most part, Beta Israel's daily practices regarding their livestock, including close relationships and feelings of attachment, were shared with their non-Jewish neighbors regardless of religious belief and affiliation. Religious distinctions were marked through these same animals, as this book will demonstrate in detail, when they passed from the living to the dead. Indeed, annual and daily routines involving close ties between humans and animals are an inherent part of the drama portrayed in this book and are thus referred to in detail.

My research throughout the years has centered primarily around ethnohistorical concerns elicited through in-depth interviews with Ethiopian Jews now living in Israel. The study attempted to reconstruct the group's daily life in Ethiopia, focusing on individuals' own depictions of life back in their homeland. The stories I heard, as well as everyday routines I witnessed, testified to the complexity of their experience. These stories included fond memories of the remote mountain villages the interviewees came from, testimonies about the intricate relations with their non-Jewish neighbors, and recitals of the internal relations among subgroups within the Beta Israel. With the dynamics of the move of this Jewish community from rural Ethiopia to Israel, dramatic changes clearly transpired. Often enough, the interpretive tools that had served the Beta Israel in forging their worldview in Ethiopia were now enlisted to explain the perplexing realities of modern-day Israel. These included formerly unimaginable experiences, such as conversion under rabbinic restrictions, moving into multistory buildings, the absence of the menstrual separation hut of the women, and perhaps above all, the newly acquired distinctiveness of the color of their bodies.

The ethnographic space that emerged between us was filled over the course of years by topics that contained scenes of everyday life from Ethiopia and from Israel. The portrayal of village life captivated both the speakers and me, creating a strong bond as we sat on soft, comfortable sofas in the living rooms of their apartments in Israel, gazing together at vistas beyond abysses of space and time. The living rooms in which we met were gradually filled with the sights and sounds of rural Ethiopia converging with present day routines. In an attempt to grasp the fine tones of their prior cultural experience, I subsequently embarked on a different form of research journey to approach the world I had for many years only heard of in as direct a fashion as possible. I traveled to northwest Ethiopia, seeking further insight into everyday life, life-cycle celebrations, and religious holidays held by the Ethiopian Jews' former neighbors.

Researching in these two different contexts, I was clearly identified as an outsider in both. In Israel the difference was modified by a common religion and language. Moreover, the *longue durée* nature of my studies of Ethiopian culture in Israel provided me with continuing contacts with community members and opportunities to participate in their evolving life. In Ethiopia, most of my encounters were spontaneous and time bound. Although my foreignness was also blatant and had to be mediated by local English translators, the detailed knowledge and relevant terminology that had so generously been given to me during my research in Israel served to bypass barriers of communication while in rural Ethiopia.

In the ethnohistorical study of group members now in Israel, my quest was for the Ethiopia within them. In-depth interviews were, to adapt Freud's well-known formulation, the available royal road to deep cultural perceptions. I continually heard detailed accounts and vivid recollections of everyday and festive rural life and of multiple interactions with Christian neighbors. While for the most part Jewish community life no longer existed in Ethiopia, I was determined to see for myself the wider world they had left behind and prepared myself for discrepancies with what I had learned.

To my astonishment, I encountered the opposite. The elaborate details that I had only heard about in the living rooms of Ethiopian Israelis now materialized in sight, sound, and odor, leaving me with a humbling gratitude to my interlocutors for the enormous efforts they had made to share with me the nuances of their original homeland. The materials gathered and vignettes recorded oscillated between Ethiopia and Israel. In addition to enduring memories of village life, my interlocutors talked about the dramatic changes that characterize their present existence. The research progressed while shifting from topic to topic, revealing a dynamic and cooperative process of building meaningful bridges—some more stable than others. Alongside the lines of research I had planned, I was surprised to discover additional topics taking center stage, whose very existence had never before come to my mind. In those precious moments, unanticipated revelations and views spontaneously emerged. Many of them are focal to this book.

The dynamics of the involved research is a concrete application of the analytical continuum between "experience-near" (concepts within the culture studied) and "experience-distant" (analytical constructs used by the researcher) understandings, as advocated by anthropologist Clifford Geertz.[12] Throughout the book the reader will encounter a number of such "experience-near" concepts, with kircha, a meat-dividing procedure, being a prime example. Whenever mentioned, it is guaranteed to elicit a smile of recognition as well as a sideways glance at how a non-Ethiopian (*ferenj*) could possibly use it. The details also cast light on "experience-distant" concepts and realms, such as the symbolism of meat, the religious framework supporting it, and the more universal psychological implications intrinsic to the human act of turning animals into food.[13]

Looking at the particulars of the relations between people and their edible domestic animals, one comes across broader themes involving a range of existential concerns.[14] For the Beta Israel and, most likely, for their Christian neighbors, meat is not just a central ingredient in their diet, but also an axis around which their very existence revolves.

The centrality of meat as an organizing medium in the lives of the Beta Israel stands at the heart of this monograph. Allusions to meat, with its seemingly endless multiplicity of life-touching nuances, constantly appeared and reappeared in conversation. These conceptualizations were not necessarily articulated in an open and direct way. As much as the materials encompassed are veiled and suffused with contradictions, their deciphering requires an ever-widening ethnographic gaze. The poetical, multivocal aspects of meat issues may be considered in dialogue with Donald Levine's approach as depicted in his seminal work on Ethiopian culture. In his study, Levine focuses on the culturally specific core idiom of the Amharic *samnawarq*, or "wax and gold," a cherished indigenous poetic form characterized by an intrinsic double meaning (outer wax and inner gold). This poetic form is creatively applied by Levine for probing into multiple arenas of Amhara life.[15]

An assemblage of diverse accounts revolving around cattle and meat in their concrete and abstract manifestations animates the following pages. A highly potent symbol, meat will be shown as capable of containing and processing—out of the transformations operated on it and through it—a series of ever-changing dynamics that touch on a wide range of issues encompassing life, death, and all that is between. In its odyssey from a living companion to a tasty dish, meat carries a baggage that spans from very concrete livestock all the way to lofty spiritual ideas.[16] The space between the two is a mélange of the human craving for meat; related practices, understandings, symbols, and folklore expressions; and much more. It is found at junctions of identity issues, the delineation of similarity and difference, inclusion and exclusion, both in Ethiopia and subsequently in postimmigration life in Israel.

Meat, both edible and metaphorical, is a stabilizing anchor available to interpret and grasp the teleportation in space and time that Ethiopian Israelis have undergone. Simultaneously, by means of this anchor, the accompanying pain and vulnerability are processed while the unbreakable connection between livestock and meat is sustained: some scenes feature the living animal while others address meat. Animals and their flesh are inseparable. Domestication as an alternative mode of sanctifying meat results in a variation of the more frequently studied cultures of sacrifice.[17] It elicited my folklore-centered ethnographic approach, inspired by everyday creativity and communication.

Rather than presenting a chronological or thematic account, this book presents a series of close-up snapshots and wide-angle ethnographic exposures. In addition, scattered throughout are a number of "selfies" taken during my stay in Ethiopia, in which themes central to the book resonate powerfully. This kaleidoscopic way of presenting meat matters is inspired by the various angles introduced by visual impressions conjured by my fieldwork. While most of these exposures were taken during in-depth interviews, others are the result of both planned and spontaneous observations and ultimately of my own ponderings over the core topics. Mediated by my wish to capture in writing these ideas and emotions, indelible memories of respectful relations between humans and animals may gain new life.

While most of the issues spoken about were vibrantly present in their consciousness, other issues arose spontaneously, surprising both my interlocutors and me. Decades after leaving Ethiopia, faded memories tended to reemerge within the ethnographic space between us. Throughout the book I made an effort to remain faithful to the unique poetics of their expressions.

The double meaning of the book's title, *Meat Matters*, acknowledges the multiplicity of issues related to meat, as well as the remarkable significance those issues hold in this community. In the life of the Beta Israel, identified as Jews in Ethiopia and subsequently as Ethiopians in Israel, space itself was dramatically transformed. Each location has had an enormous and different impact on the group's self-conception, most tellingly expressed in meat-related issues.

The path taken in this book allows for movement among a wealth of intertwined meanings that reach from the ordinary to the symbolic, spanning the concrete and the metaphoric. Originating from a wide gamut of live scenarios and remembered voices, the rich array of ethnographic materials at my disposal invited a wide-ranging and inclusive means of presentation that often appeared as genuinely poetic. Terminology derived from the field of photography kept emerging: wide-angle views and close-ups; snapshots and time exposures; fadeaways, shadows and highlights; zoomed in and zoomed out perspectives; and even selfies.[18] With these terms an overarching montage is fashioned, capturing the nuances, the contradictions, and the unexpected inherent in the subject matter. In keeping with this presentation of multiplex cultural materials and ethnographic opportunities, photographic metaphors are further employed in the separation of key sections. Analytical refractions are interspersed throughout, presented as a kind of intellectual meat repast, composed from insights and intuitions stimulated by the shifting nature of the ethnographic ingredients and my firsthand field observations.

We first look at scenes of the intimate relations between the Beta Israel and their livestock. These exposures relate directly to the centrality of animals, and especially cattle, in everyday village life in Ethiopia. Through a startling response from a Beta Israel religious leader, slaves and cows suddenly coalesce. A short account of domestic slavery leads to elaborate close-ups and fadeaway images oscillating between Ethiopia and Israel. This highly sensitive subject surfaces at different way stations as meat matters and slavery converge. Next, a series of memories related to animal slaughter and meat eating as group boundary markers in Ethiopia are shared. These are followed by a variety of scenes from Israel, in which similar practices and perceptions have been reactivated as a reaction to requirements issued by Israeli religious authorities. Shadows and highlights regarding the nexus between meat and identity that keep haunting the community in Israel are then presented. Relevant accounts taken from fieldwork in Israel and Ethiopia accompany the discussions, as do newspaper articles and digital materials. Next, a series of humorous tales involving meat issues is presented and interpreted. Their setting is modern, urban Israel, while their protagonists are tradition-bound newcomers. Once again, photography offers a framework: the tales call to mind the slapstick style of candid camera episodes. Culminating scenes return us to the centrality of the kircha spectacle, revealing the higher and even transcendental dimensions of the intimacies between cows, meat, and humans.

Notes

1. Prior to their immigration, the group was usually referred to as "Falasha." They themselves use the name "Beta Israel" ("the House of Israel") when referring to their Ethiopian past and "Ethiopian Jews" when referring to their new life in Israel. See, for example, Wurmbrand (1971); Abbink (1987, 1990); Quirin (1977, 1992).

2. The dominant version is central to the *Kebra-Nagast* (*Glory of the Kings*), a fourteenth century text, which is the national epic and legitimizes the Ethiopian Solomonic ruling dynasty.

3. The Torah (Hebrew Bible) centered, nonrabbinical religious observance of the Beta Israel is linked with their long existence in separation from other Jewish populations. See Flad (1869); Halévy (1877); Aešcoly (1943); Hess (1969); Krempel (1972, 1974); Kessler (1985); Trevisan-Semi (1985). For an account of an unsuccessful attempt to migrate from Ethiopia to Jerusalem in 1862, see Ben Dor (1987a, 5–32).

4. For the latter view, see especially Shelemay (1986); Kaplan (1990, 1992); Quirin (1992).

5. Ullendorff (1968) as well as Levine (1974, 53).

6. Biale's preface to *Cultures of the Jews* (2002) posits this idea as a foundational concept of his monumental project.

7. See Waldman (1989, 1991).

8. In particular, that of the Radbaz (acronym for Rabbi David Ibn Abi Zimra) of Egypt. See also Rapoport (1981, 201–3).

9. See, for example, Rapoport (1981, 1–14); Waldman (1989, 74–76); Kaplan (1992); Kaplan and Rosen (1993, 1994, 62).

10. The active immigration to Israel began in 1977 and continued with Operation Moses in 1984 and Operation Solomon in 1991. See also Kaplan and Rosen (1993, 35). On the Halakhic status of Ethiopian Jews, see Waldman (1989, 1991) and Corinaldi (1998). For an important critical voice and evidence regarding immigration of young Ethiopian Jews (Falashas) to Israel years before 1977, see Efrat Yardai's lecture "Who Narrates My Story?" (https://in.bgu.ac.il/cau/israeli-hope /pages/news/Ethiopian-Jews-storytelling.aspx).

11. On Operation Moses, see Parfitt (1985); Rapoport (1986); Karadawi (1991), Ben-Ezer (2002). On Operation Solomon, see Spector (2005), Weil (2007). On the

encounters between Beta Israel European missionaries in the nineteenth and early twentieth centuries, see Summerfield (2003, 17–38) and especially Kaplan (1987; 1992, 116–42; 1993). On relations between the Beta Israel and the Felasmura while still in Ethiopia, see Salamon (1999, 65–71). For an extensive historical overview with a detailed account of the Felasmura before and after their immigration to Israel, see Seeman (2003, 2009).

12.   See Geertz (1974). See also Sabar's (2020) revealing personal story on her encounter with a Beta Israel woman in Ethiopia.

13.   In his *The Raw and the Cooked* (1969), Lévi-Strauss lays the basis for a structural analysis of the nature/culture binary opposition as expressed in the preparation of food. See also Douglas on "purity and danger" (1966). For a recent exploration of the cultural history of meat consumption from 1900 onward, see Buscemi (2018). For thorough reviews of scholarship regarding religion and animal eating, see Gross (2014) and Reed (2013).

14.   See previous note. Seminal works on the complex relations between humans and cattle in Africa include Herskovits (1926a and 1926b), Evans-Pritchard (1940), and Beidelman (1966) on the Nuer, Lienhardt (1961) on the Dinka.

15.   Levine's book, *Wax and Gold* (1965), is still considered an astute and relevant analysis of traditional Ethiopian culture. See also Salamon (1995).

16.   With the growing interest in the anthropology of food and of meat eating, I wish at this point to refer to Garine (2005, 47), who summarizes his excursion into the ambiguity inherent in meat-eating states: "Consuming meat is an emotionally loaded action: its symbolic value tends to be high. It sets in motion many aspects of material and nonmaterial life. We could be tempted to refer here to the Maussian concept of 'total social phenomenon.'" This suggested totality is vividly exemplified in the present study.

17.   See Reed (2013) for an insightful overview of sacrificial ideas and practices.

18.   The use of photographic terminology is shared with Kirin Narayan, who focuses on "wide angles" and "close-ups" in her stimulating book on ethnographic writing, *Alive in the Writing* (2012, 37–40).

Enduring Exposures

Everyday Bonding with Creatures

Avraham "Abera" Pardo fled nearly thirty years ago from the village in north-western Ethiopia where he had spent most of his life. He cannot cease to long for it. Today, as he surpasses the age of ninety, he is well settled in a spacious apartment in one of the new neighborhoods adjacent to Jerusalem, where he is surrounded by his loving and well-established family. Nevertheless, memories of village life continue to permeate his daily routine.[1] As he sits on an upholstered chair in his modern, brightly lit living room, he invites his unforgotten farm creatures to visit: a large block of white paper on his lap, he paints again and again, using vivid colors, chickens, goats, sheep, oxen, and his favorite of all, cows. I came several times to talk with him about his paintings. Avraham's memories of Ethiopia fill the room both in words and images. Each individual animal merits its own colors and distinctive facial expression. In most of the pictures, the animals are positioned in one direction, as if making their way home after having spent a peaceful day in the pasture.[2]

Toward the end of one of my visits, I had an unanticipated experience. In the midst of recalling his hasty departure with his family for Israel, Avraham leaned back in his chair, lowered his eyes, and to my astonishment, impersonated his beloved cow's extended, baleful mooing. By means of his own soulful voice, he seemed to unite with his crying cows, sounding their moans and his own in tandem. His wife, hearing his lament, joined in.[3] On returning to human speech, Avraham explained that the sounds echo those of his precious cows, lamenting their mutual, imminent separation. The impromptu concert of mourning revealed without doubt that despite leaving the animals behind, Avraham and his wife carried them to their new life in Israel. Apparently, even after more than thirty years, there has been no substitute for the deep relationships they had with their beloved livestock. In fact, regardless of all the comfort of their present life, something very essential to them has remained unobtainable.

The cries of Avraham's beloved animals echoed in the modern living room, and for a brief moment it was as if we had time traveled to his home village. Hearing these sounds, I suddenly realized that I had failed to appreciate fully what it means to be an owner of livestock and have animals be such an intimate part of one's daily life.[4] I knew I had to go back and reexamine what I had taken to be mundane practices of rural life. These everyday relations, more than I had ever grasped until this spontaneous drama, were the bedrock of practically every issue raised during my research with the Beta Israel.

While for the Beta Israel in Ethiopia, the loss of a beloved cow to death, slaughter, or sale was a familiar experience, nothing could have prepared them for the total demise of their cattle when they turned their back on their home village and took the first step toward Jerusalem. Their departure was often done in an Exodus-like haste, leaving very little time to sell the herd or even hand it over to neighbors.[5] It was this specific moment of unanticipated separation that generated the colorful painted images and lamenting sounds still being recreated, whether tangibly or in imagination, in so many apartments in Israel. The deep longing for the cows left behind was invariably communicated to me by means of elaborate descriptions of an individual, beloved cow: her humble gaze; her smooth skin; her fresh, warm milk; her manure that fertilized the crops and was used for building as well as fuel for cooking and heating; and eventually, mentioned with much respect, the tastiness of her flesh. All this was readily called to mind by many of my Ethiopian-born friends. The underpinning of this bond is demonstrated in the following quote: "More than anything, we miss cows. Wealth is measured in Ethiopia according to cows. The cow is also a type of exchange, as we use them for transactions, and that makes them a status symbol of wealth. Also, the milk that we used to drink. And when they get old, there is the meat that we eat. Their body is rich with meat."

In the words of another Ethiopian born Israeli, "The cattle is your existence. There is plowing. The cow gives milk; she also gives birth and so it is a developing property. An investment, a dividend. Even more than this: there, there is no monthly salary. So it's plowing. The seeds that you sow, and the produce that comes, and the cows that give birth, this is your monthly salary."

Yet another interviewee explained:

> They [the cows] value more, they are expensive. The cow, she gives tremen-
> dous rewards to our life: her milk, her dung, even her urine. To everything
> she has a tremendous contribution. Her milk, I'll tell you about her milk.
> That's really important. And after she gets too old for milk, then we eat her
> meat. That is to say that she has in fact not just a double or triple contribu-
> tion, but a fourfold contribution. And when she gets old and we eat her,
> there is also her hide that is used as a bed covering. We had one cow that
> gave birth to seven. So from one came out seven—do you understand what
> that means?

In fact, even after hearing so many convincing testimonies, I was not sure that I fully understood what they meant. The profitability was easy to see. The cattle, and especially the cow, is perceived as a living bank, with its accounts being very concrete and its profits publicly displayed. But the depth of the sentiments remained unclear. I could very well hear expressions of love and honor that were contained within every sentence about cows. These sentiments, undi-minished by time and place, posed a challenge for interpretation. The first step in grappling with them obviously required a close examination of the daily relations of Beta Israel with their livestock (see fig. 1.1).

What I heard from Avraham and many others was not just yearning but also their firsthand detailed knowledge available in precise language and vivid im-ages. A family's herd, called *amga*, included edible animals such as goats, sheep, and cattle and working animals such as mules, donkeys, and horses.

Name giving personalized the special relationship with one's cattle in the Ethiopian village, and no other animal was given a distinct and individual name. Names were given to calves, oxen, bulls, and cows, and these names, I was told, were mostly connected with their external appearance—size, color, patterns, and other special markings—as well as distinctive behavioral char-acteristics and temperaments.[6] The people with whom I spoke extolled their cattle, and especially the cows, for responding to their personal names.

Children as young as three began to interact with the family livestock. From the beginnings of their lives as shepherds, they learned to recognize the voice of every individual animal. The youngest, both boys and girls, tagged along with their older siblings and the neighbors' children and learned the essentials of shepherding by observation and casual guidance.[7] At the dawn of each day, when the oxen were taken out to work in the fields, the children went out to

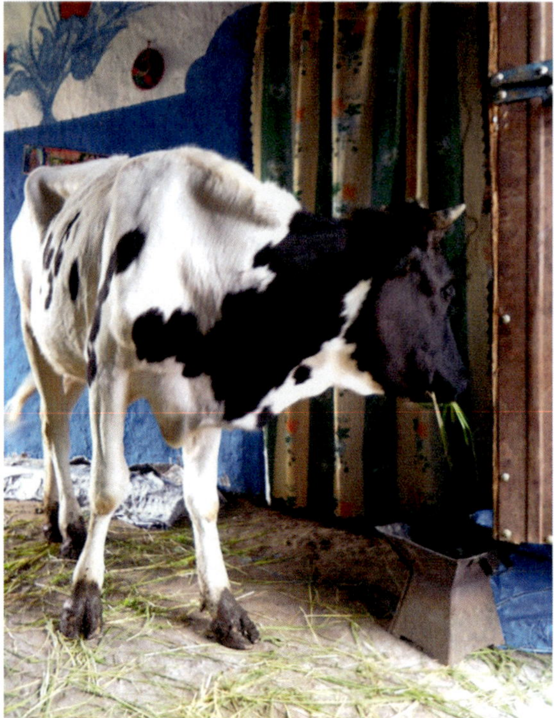

Figure 1.1. A family cow munches from decorative holiday grass strewn over the living room floor, Bahir Dar vicinity, 2015. Photo: Hagar Salamon.

the pasture with the animals. The children were expected to make sure the animals ate and drank properly, while keeping all animals from danger and escorting them safely home at the end of the day. Over the course of the day, there were moments that required great care and attention, as well as times for play and relaxation. At the place of watering, there was a gathering of numerous herds, and the atmosphere was relaxed and less restrained. However, on departure there was apt to be commotion, and great care had to be taken to prevent confusion among the different herds. Enormous attention was required to make sure that no animal was lost or taken away by mistake.

Children learned the animals' preferences by experience. They acquired knowledge as to the special grasses each liked and where those grasses could best be found. They learned each animal's favorite watering places and their unique qualities. If they had the chance, the children would bathe and swim where the animals were bathing and take a nap or play together while the animals were resting and ruminating. At the same time, constant diligence was necessary, because water sources could be dangerous. They could be polluted, contain irritating insects, and especially, as I was repeatedly told, carry leeches. These could be swallowed while drinking and latch on inside the animal's throat, causing great suffering and even endangering its life. Despite all the precautions, it was necessary for at least some of the older children to become experts at the emergency procedures required for leech extraction.

Even while still very young, the children gradually became adept at providing personal care to the animals under their charge—including the recognition of injuries and diseases. In serious cases, they were of course obliged to seek out help immediately and could approach any adult in the vicinity, in what was termed by the interviewees "mutual responsibility" or "cooperative guarantees," regardless of familial or religious affiliation.

Another often-mentioned task demanding constant alertness was that of keeping one's own herd from grazing in cultivated fields, whether they belonged to the family or to others. A mishap here would require familial apology and sometimes even a monetary guarantee against future occurrences. Some cases might involve accusations, arguments, and litigations. To prevent such confrontations, dogs were relied on to assist with herding as well as guarding the house from wild animal and human intruders.

At the end of each day, the herd was brought back to the family compound. On reaching it, each animal went on its own to its assigned pen, which was usually adjacent to the family house for protection from thieves and from night attacks by jackals, wolves, or hyenas. While goats and sheep dwelled together in one pen, as did the donkeys and horses, the cattle were kept in a separate pen lest they harm other livestock with their horns. In a subsequent section, the topic of household slavery will be introduced, and we will meet others who often shared these pens.

All in all, herding was a complex task that required from young children an early development of responsibility, abiding attention, and ever-expanding knowledge of the animals' needs and habits. Carried out along with neighboring children, shepherding served as a kind of school for life. In rural Ethiopia, where schools were once scarce, much of an individual's education practically relied on what was gleaned from shepherding. The animals' daily routines and those of the children became synchronized with one another in an inseparable manner.

In light of all this, it is not surprising that many of the most popular children's games were engaged with or involved imagining domestic animals, especially cattle.[8] Older children created games with real animals, such as contests between two teams (called *aura berie siwagu*, "when the oxen fight") in which two oxen, each representing one side, were stimulated to fight one another. Younger children enjoyed making clay models of cattle, especially cows, so that in their games, they could simulate the wide-ranging options available to grownups by way of their cows.

Game playing was just part of a learning web by means of observation, in which the children were constantly watching and caring for their flocks. Their efforts and responsibilities provided them with insights and understandings that would last a lifetime whether in Ethiopia or faraway Israel.

In many areas where the Beta Israel lived, there was period of a few months every year in which the children and the cattle moved together to a grazing area at a distance from home. This period, called *karat*, took place in the rainy season (June to September in this part of the globe), during which the animals were not needed for any work in the fields: the soil is muddy and therefore difficult to move around. In addition, the crops, nearly ripe, needed to be protected from the grazing herd. The animals, accompanied by the adolescent boys, were taken to a remote uncultivated area and remained there for the entire period. The children moved to a temporary *gojo* (hut), which had to be renewed every year. Free to graze, the animals were expected to return fatter and stronger after the karat period. For both animals and youngsters, the karat was a special moratorium, when normal everyday tasks were in abeyance. These periods were described, however, in ambivalent terms. The youngsters were for the most part without adult supervision. They could milk the animals at their leisure and freely enjoy the milk, even if they had to save some of it for their families. Most of the shepherding tasks were not required, and the children were free to play as if "in a summer camp," to use one of the interviewee's expressions. At the same time, being away from the protection of home made the potential dangers of wild animal attacks terrifyingly present. Adults would visit frequently and even spend the night with the children. They would bring the children food, check on the herds, and take home containers of milk.

This special period deserves, in my opinion, further study in relation to coming of age for boys in rural Ethiopia. The materials dealt with here are another layer in the depiction of the close relations between humans and livestock that

I am seeking to grasp. The tales of the karat portray a picture of Edenic freedom from boundaries for the children and from enclosures for the animals. Milk was freely available, and there was an ever-present sense of being in the wilderness, where wild animals roam.

As the youngsters matured, they entered more serious working relationships with the cattle, especially the males. Boys and (mainly) male cattle worked together in the field, primarily plowing and threshing, heavy tasks for which the cattle's efforts were indispensable. The division of the male cattle into bulls and oxen reflected their expected contributions for work in the field, for procreation, and for meat.

A few males in the herd were kept as bulls to fertilize the cows, while the majority underwent castration. The harsh procedure was public and well known to the people I spoke with; it was done by local practitioners whose expertise basically entailed the safe smashing of the bulls' testicles between two stones. Following this distressing but rather routine procedure, these animals, now oxen, better sustained their stamina and bodily strength for the taxing work in the fields. In addition, I was told, the monetary value of oxen surpassed that of bulls.

The life of most male cattle was divided, then, into two phases. In the first phase, the male fulfilled its procreative potential while still working in the field. In the second phase, after having reached a certain age, it was castrated, sacrificing virility in exchange for the maintenance of physical strength.

When talking about cattle, people use a plethora of terms to specify the stages of their development. These terms are based on both age and fertility and are thus indicative of the centrality of these criteria in the ongoing relations between people and their cattle. While the initial two stages of development are named identically for males and females, a sharp differentiation based on gender is employed as the cattle mature. In trying to grasp the possible implications of this terminology, I suggest that the newborn and young calves, whether male or female, still under the care of their mothers, are in the category of a "protected promise," a stage that does not tolerate human intervention. Thus, both male and female cattle from birth to three or four months of age are called *enbossa,* and from about four months to two or three years of age the term used for both is *tija.* After age three, however, gender differentiation appears: the male is called *weifen* and the female *gider*. The gider is generally spared slaughter, mostly on account of her not yet having given birth or on the chance she might be pregnant. From age five onward, the uncastrated male is known as *korma*. The korma has reached the stage for being trained to bear a yoke and work together with an already trained and experienced ox. Once castrated, regardless of age, the ox is called *sanga*. If the gider is barren, she becomes a *shehar*. As I came to learn, the flesh of a shehar is considered extremely tasty. Regarding each named animal, there are standard expectations and avoidances in relation to plowing as well as suitability for slaughtering. For example, the enbossa and tija are protected and will not be slaughtered for any reason. The korma is also protected, unless there are good reasons for the owner to slaughter it.[9]

In a highly sensitive close-up, the painful training procedures for korma were recalled:

> When you [as owner of cattle] train a young korma to do the farming tasks and pull the *maresha* (plow), the owner will tell about it to his community. This will help him to find another ox from his neighbors to do the work for both of them.[10] So he is announcing good news. So, when you announce it, it means that I trained my korma to go for farming. He is now not a simple ox; it is a working ox. It is difficult for about fifteen days. They have to put the yoke on their neck, and so in the beginning you usually just put it on the young korma's neck. He doesn't like it, so he tries to get rid of it, but he can't, so you just leave it on the korma for fifteen or more days. Finally, the owner will bring the trained ox, which already accepts his burden and yoke, and tie them together (because the yoke is actually made for two oxen) to pull the maresha. Of course, the korma doesn't simply pull the maresha; the farmer uses the *jiraf* (whip). It is very painful and causes wounds, so the newly trained oxen are forced to accept to pull the maresha. After a while even the sound of the jiraf threatens it and forces it to behave. [See fig. 1.2.]

The elicitation of the oxen's work potential is divided between sweet talk and the whip. At the time of plowing, the farmer will sing special songs, repeat certain rhymes, quote some proverbs, or whistle a catchy tune to relax the beast and make it work smoothly. There is a customary poetic repertoire connected to each kind of work. This contrasts with milking, when it is apparently more effective to remain silent and have a quiet togetherness. Singing while involved

Figure 1.2. Two oxen plowing, directed by a jiraf-wielding farmer, Tigray vicinity, 2018. Photo: Hagar Salamon.

with the working cattle was explained: "This is just like when you talk or sing to a baby. You praise him and flatter him for its beautiful hair, eyes, smile, and so on. So, to the oxen or cows you speak similarly, praising them in words and songs."

These sweet words were accompanied by the ever-present whip, and this balance was utilized by the farmers in a subtly elaborated manner. These were the two extremes marking the course of the threshing process, laden with a variety of managing methods. In addition to the gentle ways of fostering obedience by means of songs and words of personalized endearment, the farmer must have at the ready a real whip as well. It is this instrument that enables him to assert his mastery. In recollecting the specific steps in the process, one of my interviewees described in detail how ten to fifteen oxen were usually required for this painstaking work:

> You want them to continue working without a break, so what do you do to them? You muzzle them in the very beginning, during the first hour, and

you make them go round and around to begin to separate the grain from its chaff. Then you release the muzzle, to let them taste a little bit of the grain. Then you say to them: You are my oxen; I bless you while I make you go around threshing that you will go around and get my crop for me. This way of speaking connects to a familiar proverb that we say: "Tell the poor person that there is *injera,* and he will cross forty-four rivers to get it." When we say this proverb in regard to the oxen, it's because if he knows that there is a lot of food waiting for him, he'll bear up under the heavy burden of the yoke and work to his utmost.

Another verbal way of motivating the oxen was by threat. For example, amid recollecting the threshing, my Ethiopian Israeli interviewee suddenly recalled a type of "conversation" he engaged in with his oxen:

"Look at how I am working, that's how I want you to work! If you don't work like that, I will sell you to a Muslim, a Muslim that will immediately take you to slaughter." Why [am I saying this to them]? Because just like ISIS today,[11] there [in Ethiopia] too, the Muslims slaughter all the time. They slaughter a lot because they are often merchants and have a lot of money, so they buy [animals] and slaughter.

These two verbal whips can be seen as aesthetic formulations of the unity of purpose between the owner and his oxen. In brief, they say, "With me, you have your life, and without me you are only meat." The personification of the oxen indeed facilitates this kind of conversation, in which the different possible forms of its body—working beast, starving or satiated creature, or block of meat—are presented as viable choices for the oxen.

Giving the oxen a hint of the purpose of the hard work at the beginning of the threshing and an intimation of the outcome of their mutual efforts created a bond. It was all about imagining partnership. The oxen and farmers were thus united, so to speak, in working for a satisfying reward that appealed to each of them. Nonetheless, the potential for recalcitrance and even rebelliousness from the oxen remained an omnipresent concern, a shadow hovering over their daily interaction. It seems that despite the already foregone conclusion of the struggle between men and beast, its results, so to speak, had to be reenacted and its concrete manifestations reimposed. The overt need for domination by the male owner over his oxen, so different from the affectionate attitude to cows, plays itself out not only in moments of concrete resistance but rather as a matter of routine.

Notes

1. Although Avraham Pardo was ninety years old at the time of our meeting and was portraying for me events that had occurred many years before, I found his recollections detailed, sharp, and closely matching descriptions of other interviewees with whom I spoke over the years. Throughout my research, I am searching for the ethnographic landscape embedded in memory.

2. On ethnographic memories represented in paintings, see Kirshenblatt and Kirshenblatt-Gimblett (2007). In that case, however, and unlike Pardo, the paintings were elicited by his daughter, the ethnographer.

3. Avraham's captivating reenactment performed in an apartment in Israel resonates with Lienhardt's account of the Dinka reenactments of the sounds and movements of their bulls and oxen: "The stamping and cries of the men are stylizations of the sounds and vigorous movements of bulls and oxen" (Lienhardt 1961, 17).

4. These strong emotional connections are highlighted in some of the most influential ethnographies of pastoral and semipastoral groups of the Horn of Africa and East Africa. Any discussion of the elaborate relations between humans and livestock in East Africa calls up Herskovits's seminal "cattle complex" formulation from 1926, where he demonstrates how prestige and morality are displayed in connection with cattle ownership, thus stretching far beyond purely economic considerations. His insight was incorporated into the classical ethnographies of Evans-Pritchard on the Nuer (1940), as well as of Lienhardt on the Dinka in the Sudan (1961). Their fieldwork was carried out among tribes that live in zones that border Ethiopia. More recently, the complexity that transpires in such an intimate setting between a human group and their cattle is described by Abbink (2003), who attempts to explain the tremendous ambivalence that such proximity creates for the Suris in southwestern Ethiopia. The symbiotic relations described in this example are so extreme that groups cannot be defined as separate entities. The article describes the nurturing and closeness, but also the cruel slaughtering routines and sacrifices. In an attempt to understand this paradox, the writer locates the tension between conceptions of closeness and equality in the relationship and the aspect of economic, social, and emotional expediency: "The Suri, a pastoral group, view their animals as an extension, or better overlap, of human social groups, enhancing their survival chances in their difficult environment and enriching their society. . . . Cattle are thus the medium and metaphor of human sociality . . . but they are also sacrificed, and in that context are the prime vehicle for abreacting the problems emerging in human social life, and indirectly for connecting to supernatural forces" (Abbink 2003, 346).

5. The travails of the journey from Ethiopia to Israel via Sudan are often compared with the biblical Exodus in personal and public narratives of the community.

For a detailed documentation and an analysis of these narratives see Ben-Ezer (2002).

6. Giving personal names to domestic animals in general and to cattle in particular is, of course, known in other cultural contexts, and in some groups in the Horn of Africa, especially among pastoralists, relations are far more intricate. Lienhardt, referring to the "obsession" of the Dinka with the colors and patterns of their cattle, especially oxen, writes about the "vast Dinka vocabulary referring to cattle, and particularly to the varieties of their coloring and shading in their almost innumerable blends and configurations. The interest and, one might almost say, obsession that produces and develops this vocabulary is not primarily practical in nature." In what follows, Lienhardt describes in detail the nuanced and highly elaborated cattle taxonomies that bring together facets of the interrelations between the two species and are used in their perception of their world—natural and social, communal and personal (1961, 10–11). For a study on the close relationship of the Hamer people of the South Omo region with their chosen ox see, Dubosson (2014). His study shows how personal desires are projected by means of the body of a favorite ox (*errawak*). For a more general examination of "companion species," see Haraway (2003).

7. See also Poluha (2007), especially pages 84–85, who describes the world of children in urban and rural Ethiopia.

8. For the wider Ethiopian context, see Jirata (2012, 2017).

9. Both Evans-Pritchard (1940) and Beidelman (1966), in their close examinations of the relations of the Nuer and their cattle, relate the specificities of the different categories within the herds. Especially relevant to the categories mentioned is Beidelman's discussion of the parallels between cattle and humans (1966, 459–63).

10. On neighbors borrowing oxen to assist in plowing and harvesting, along with established agreements in certain rural areas, see the in-depth historical study of McCann (1995, 79–80). For a more recent depiction of household social and economic organization, specifically in Tigray, see Bauer (1977).

11. This interview was conducted in the summer of 2014, when the world news reports were replete with images of ISIS's gruesome human executions. This interviewee related these images to the Ethiopian way of slaughtering livestock. The original threat was related to the perceived habits of Muslims in Ethiopia, which are being reinterpreted and reinforced by present-day news.

Zooming In

Creaturely Sentiments

The following snapshot was taken during an interview with a Beta Israel *qes*[1]:

> A barya is like a cow or like a donkey . . . he works like a cow. He prays to
> God and all he says is that God is right. . . . He thinks that in heaven there
> is lots of milk, lots of cows . . . all they say is "barukh"[2] . . . [laughing]. He
> doesn't know how to pray—he just says bo! bo! bo! . . . They tell him that
> if he isn't good [here, the speaker almost chokes on his laughter], he'll be
> beaten in heaven.[3]

I found his choice of animal images, coupled with a demeaning laugh, enigmatic and yet intrinsically disconsoling. The wider and deeper significance of all this seeped only gradually into my consciousness. Faced with God, milk, heaven, beatings, and above all, what seemed to me a sheepish yet naively malevolent laughter, I initially believed that this collection of images was merely an expression of one individual's decadence and malice. However, in further interviews I heard expressions that put the qes's words into a broader context.

Over the years, Ethiopians in Israel talked to me with a unique mixture of caution and enthusiasm about themselves as owners of other people. My acquaintance with the topic of slavery in Ethiopia and its related cultural understandings thus began very far from its actual context.[4] Gradually it became shockingly clear to me that these interviewees were referring to a hierarchical and exploitative system of slavery that had existed in Ethiopia. In further interviews I learned about its everyday manifestations and related racial perceptions.[5] Some of the Beta Israel, like their non-Jewish neighbors, owned slaves, who as a group were called *barya*. In Ethiopia, the term simultaneously denoted employment, status, and origin and was juxtaposed against the term *choa*, which designated a free human assumed to be refined and civilized.[6]

Among the interviewees was a smattering of ex-masters as well as ex-slaves. When the Beta Israel immigrated to Israel, choa and barya came together. Some of the barya had been freed years earlier. Others, who in Ethiopia lived as slaves within the family compound, were brought by the choa with the hope that they would continue to serve them in the new land. But with the transition to Israel, a dramatic change occurred in the lives of the barya, who, as citizens of the new country, were considered no different from other members of the Ethiopian community. Life in Israel radically altered power relations, but at the same time, the mark of the barya's different status within the community lingered. Within the Israeli Ethiopian community, although attitudes are gradually changing, former slaves and their offspring to this day are marked as different, especially by the older generation.[7] Older people still resist any desire of their children and grandchildren to marry them, and great importance is placed on preserving barya genealogy and separateness. The distinction is maintained within the Beta Israel community but essentially unknown to the larger Israeli society.

According to the masters' accounts, the barya were generally purchased at local markets during the pre-abolition period, but accounts of kidnappings and slave stealing presented as adventurous exploits also prevail.[8] Even after the official abolition of slavery in Ethiopia, the prohibition of the slave trade in 1924, and the antislavery proclamation made in 1931 by Emperor Haile Selassie,[9] some barya remained a de facto part of family property, to be bequeathed from one generation to the next. The system of enslavement—in which Ethiopian Jews and their Christian and Muslim neighbors employed household slaves who lived with them, for the most part in unadulterated subjugation—was intertwined with a racist hierarchy constructed primarily through an imagined differentiation in skin color. Even though in actuality there may be few if any obvious physical differences between a choa and a barya, the choa's strong desire to separate and delineate the barya suggests the magnitude of the perceived threat posed by blurring the boundaries. Choa interviewees shared with me traditional mythological explanations for the differences between the choa and the barya.[10]

In the many hesitant stories I heard related to master-slave hierarchies, cows figured prominently.[11] In these stories it is not the cow "elevated" to the human, rather the human "lowered" to the bovine. Reference to these changing hierarchies appear throughout the book as ex-masters and ex-slaves now living in Israel as equal citizens speak about cows in their efforts to flesh out repressed memories of slavery. These disparate perspectives invite us to decode the specific vocabulary associated with the twilight zone that lies between those considered human and those regarded as nonhuman in discussions of slavery in Ethiopia.[12]

My acquaintance with Abba Legesse's extended household was made through Mammit, who was twenty-eight when I met her.[13] Born a slave in Ethiopia, she immigrated to Israel at the age of thirteen. Her mother, Terengo, and maternal aunt Habtesh were raised in the household of their ex-master, Abba Legesse, and his wife, their ex-mistress, Sosana.[14] Of all Terengo's children, only Mammit and her sister Muchit, about ten years younger, are still alive. Another woman, Twawosh, was the eldest of the female slaves who lived in the household. Known by all as Grandma, she was brought to Abba Legesse's compound as part of the dowry (*macha*) of Sosana. It was through my close friendship with Mammit that I had the privilege of gaining access to the often painful stories of Abba Legesse's and Sosana's baryas. Mammit recalls:

> Mother slept outside in a kind of booth near the entrance. It's a kind of booth that's open on the side . . . in the place where my mother slept, not much rain got in because there was a piece of tin of some kind [serving as a roof]. Next to them are cows and donkeys and also chickens—you name it, it's there. Really, we miss living there. There are cows who like you, and they come close only to you and not to anyone else. And once, when I was little, an animal kicked me far, far away [laughs]. [The place] where my mother sleeps in the booth is outside, next to all the animals. There's no door to the booth—it's open on both sides. . . . The animals are next to it but not inside. They don't go in there. When a man comes to my mother, he approaches the place she is sleeping. There are no doors to her booth.

Once again Mammit reenacts her master's denigrating phraseology, shifting between his and her own perspective:

> Abba Legesse would always say to his children, "What will they [the barya] do to you? What will you do to them? What? Will you drink their blood? Will you eat their flesh? Hit them so that they'll work—otherwise, when they grow up, you'll see what they'll do to you." . . . That's what Abba Legesse would tell his children. He would tell them that when we're big, maybe we'll get out of

there; we'll take control of them. Maybe we'll do something, so let them hit us while we're young. Let them have control of us. That's what he would say.

It is apparent that Abba Legesse's education of his children and young grandchildren included clear instructions for dealing with the barya, particularly the guideline that beating was a tool of the trade, a means of domestication, and an absolute necessity. The mention of the barya's inedible flesh and undrinkable blood, images that were repeated in other narrative contexts, raises the comparison between barya and cattle.[15] Although based on the distinction between them, the very comparison suggests its relevance. The expressions of fear projected onto Abba Legesse by Mammit are illuminating. From her current, fundamentally different status, Mammit revives the metaphors and images of flesh and blood that on a daily basis sustained the management of oppression. The nature of these expressions is indicative, in my reading, of the ambivalence in the choa's attitude toward the barya: relating to them as if cattle while at the same time obviously aware they are not. Questioning the sameness of barya and cow bore the potential to shake the foundations of the exploitative order. Thus, in slaveholding choa families, subservience had to be routinely inflicted on the barya by means of regular beatings so both the barya and the young choa children would properly internalize the hierarchy. Mammit relates:

> She [Sosana] says to her children: "You have to beat them." . . . Even when you do all the work you get beaten. With us, it's in the house, inside the family . . . you grow up with them, and they give you hell, and you don't know where to turn. You don't know who you are. Everyone there is the same, kicking our legs, shouting at us: "Go away, you—scram." And beatings of the head with a stick, with fists, with whatever they could find. It was full of blood. We're like a cow to them.

Mammit's account exposes cruelty and pain as well as her own incredulousness at the central experience of inexplicable violence with which she was treated. She conveys this experience through the image of the cow. Abba Legesse's reference to the barya's flesh, as recounted by Mammit, resonates with an episode relating to Sosana's bloody biting assaults on the baryas under her command, which will be recounted elsewhere.

A mandatory part of every young man's education is mastering the tricks of the trade necessary for assuring that the routine display of domination between him and his oxen is inviolate and always results in human victory. Thus, foremost among the skills that a young man aspires to obtain is the adroit use of the whip: it serves him as his primary instrument to overcome the contention liable to arise when a relatively frail human being acts to dominate a huge, powerful beast. Initial expertise requires knowing how to use the whip as a source of "martial music"—to snap it overhead in the precise way that emits a range of intimidating sounds capable of convincing the oxen to obey the commands of the owner unhesitatingly. On the occasions for which it is deemed necessary to apply direct lashings, the owner has to be capable of skillfully modulating the movement of his arm so that the animal would feel the sting of the whip yet not be seriously injured or overly incensed by the contact.

The necessity of a decisive victory in every battle or rivalry between owners and their oxen is central to the inherent power relations between them. The complexity of these relations is embodied in the remarkable crafting of the whip itself. To my astonishment, along with using the dried skin of the slaughtered beast for the length of the whip, the animal's dried sexual organ, known as *ye-jiraf ras* (lit. "the head of the whip"), serves as a joint to increase its flexibility and strength. I had been told about this custom in a matter-of-fact fashion and with a sheerly functional explanation by my Israeli Ethiopian friends shortly before I left for fieldwork in Ethiopia. I must admit that this tool was beyond my imagination, and I honestly didn't expect to come across one in its materiality. Oddly enough, it was one of the first items I documented on reaching the market in Gondar (see fig. 2.1 and 2.2). While visiting a stall specializing in hides, I noticed, attached to a wooden pillar, a handful of leather whips, each with an unobtrusive, flexible ring joint. Asking about the flexible ring, I was told—again in a matter-of-fact tone—that this was the ye-jiraf ras, and that without being overly explicit, everyone knows its origin. People kept explaining that this part of the animal's body was especially appropriate for maximizing the impact of the whip. I wasn't sure I accurately grasped their depictions and didn't dare to probe further. Only some time later, after actually seeing the whip in use, did the extent of its symbolic implications strike me. These implications could be taken as an example of the coalescence of what was initially identified by James Frazer as sympathetic (or metaphoric) magical logic and contagious (or metonymic) magical logic, a combination of the power of similarity and the power of contiguity. The organ of potency of an ox is taken into the hands of the human master to exert control over the working capacity of another ox.

When my Ethiopian friends discussed their reliance on their cattle, they never forgot to mention the beneficial uses of cattle dung and urine. In their villages, dung was indispensable. It was used to insulate the walls of the huts against inclement weather and as fuel for cooking and heating. The cattle's

Figure 2.1. The jiraf and ye-jiraf ras, Gondar market, 2015. Photo: Hagar Salamon.

Figure 2.2. Displaying a ye-jiraf ras in use, Bahir Dar vicinity, 2015. Photo: Hagar Salamon.

Figure 2.3. Stretching cattle hides, Gondar vicinity, 2015. Photo: Hagar Salamon.

manure was therefore diligently collected, dried, and preserved, mostly by girls and women. When recalling these practices, my interlocutors would typically exclaim about the sweet smell of the droppings. While they associated the good odor with the cattle's diet of natural grass, it also was a way of praising their homegrown Ethiopian cattle. Their lauding of the sweet odor was yet another overt indication of the longing they sustained for their animals.

The urine was also appreciated for its many uses, especially in the processing of hides and the preparation of leather products such as mattresses, baby carriers, and saddles, as well as other household items. Cattle urine was essential in the transformation of animal skins into usable, soft leather. As part of a highly elaborated process to enable the removal of hair and blemishes, the hides were immersed in cattle urine, which was collected in a special vessel and mixed with highly acidic seeds and toxic fruits. The treated hide was then stretched between pegs above the ground (see fig. 2.3).

Of all the bounty a cow offers, milk was among the most highly valued by the Beta Israel. In the areas where the Beta Israel lived, only cow's milk was drunk (the milk of sheep and goats was considered inedible and even damaging). Milking drew the animal and its owner into a physically close and attentive interaction, which constantly renewed the emotional bond the owner felt with the cow. Cow's milk and its related products—butter, yogurt, and cheese—are basic components of the daily Ethiopian menu.[16] Procuring the milk requires great sensitivity to and familiarity with the habits and moods of each cow. I was told again and again how the milk production is dependent on subtle coordination among milkers, cows, and calves. Calves are kept at home, separate from the cows sent to graze. Apart from their mothers all day long, they are eager to suck when the cows return at the end of the herding day. The owner takes priority over the milk, yet it will not flow unless the calf is brought close to its mother and begins to suck. In recounting the milking scene, the interviewees described the dynamics of this daily calf-cow separation and reunion and the precise combination of watchfulness and force it requires (see fig. 2.4). Invariably, listening to the descriptions, I was struck by the depth and vitality of the emotions engendered by this tightly managed form of ongoing breastfeeding. I heard about preferred body positions for doing the milking, the careful manipulations used to keep the calf both close to and apart from its mother, the hush that was conducive to bringing out the flow of milk, and finally the overall enchantment that imbued the rush of the warm milk into the decorated gourds or, recently, plastic urns awaiting it. This skill and attention were necessary to prevent the cow from withholding its milk, which was a constant concern.

Descriptions were detailed, graphic, and often given with dramatic gestures. The sounds of the reunion of the cow with her calf were recreated, with emphasis on how eager they were to be joined in nursing. The calf's initial suckling was watched carefully, until white, warm drippings were visible around its mouth. This was the sign for the owner to immediately pull the calf away from its mother's udder, while keeping it close to her, so she could keep licking it. Only in this way, by sustaining the intimate closeness between them, would the mother continue to express her precious milk.

Once enough milk for the household was collected, the calf was allowed to return to its suckling. For the next few evening hours, the two remained together for a period of nuzzling and cuddling and more suckling. Before bedtime, however, they were usually separated once again. The calves were then either brought into the main house, where they would sleep along with the family members, or placed in a separate guarded pen to protect them from possible attacks by wild animals. This arrangement prevented the calf from

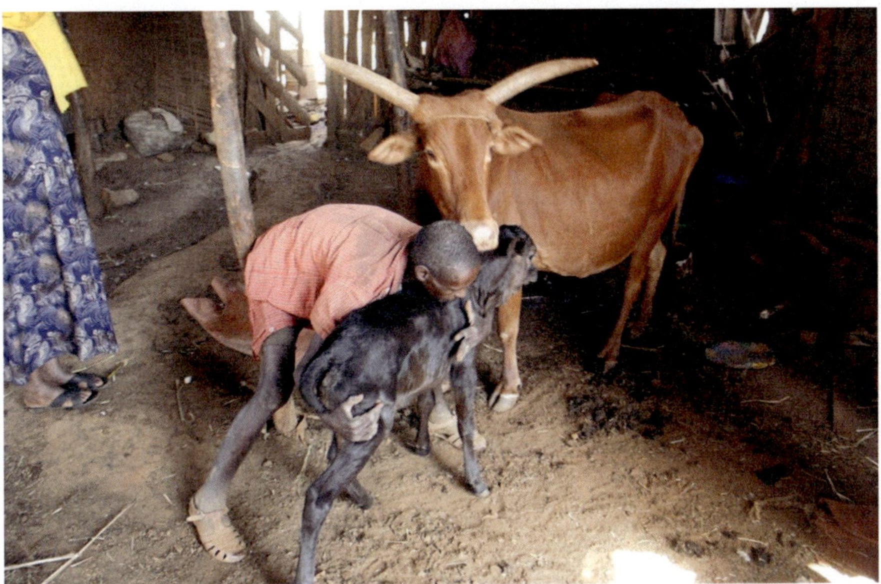

Figure 2.4. Placing the calf in front of its mother to stimulate milking, Bahir Dar vicinity, 2015. Photo: Hagar Salamon.

suckling all night, which might cause the cow to have a shortage of milk the next morning.

All this was shared with great emotion by the Beta Israel, as if sharing memories of beloved family members. The obvious mother-child features of this interaction stood out, despite the tellers' own repeated invasion into the intimate relations between cow and calf. Altogether, milking made a lasting impression and seemed to have become intertwined with the tellers' own parental inclinations.

Again, the voice of Mammit resonates:

> And they also took the milk. My mother, when she had a baby and she had milk, they also had a baby granddaughter, so they took her milk for their baby.[17] Our baby doesn't interest them. Also, all their babies were always on our backs. We were the only ones who carried them. My mother's sister, my aunt, also had a lot of milk, so they would take hers for their children. And even though she did all that, they would still beat her.

While recounting these details, two of my interviewees spontaneously recalled situations in which a calf died. Given the importance of the calf in the production of milk, this created a double loss: not only of the calf itself, but also of its mother's milk. To deal with this challenging circumstance, a dramatic solution was applied. They would skin the hide of the deceased calf, preserve it, and stuff it with specially prepared straw so that it could be restored to its original shape. The resulting model had to be realistic enough to convince the bereaved cow that her calf was still there, waiting for her milk. This deception, if well designed, might get an additional few weeks of milk until the mother cow caught on to the ruse. The emotional drama of this revelatory moment was portrayed vividly by the teller of the story: "She would get angry, stomping her hooves, kicking, shaking her horns and attempting to attack. Then it was clear that it was time to take away the stuffed calf."

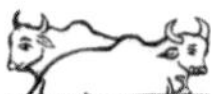

The lifelong attentiveness to the mood and disposition of the cows created a nuanced communication between people and their animals. Consider the following testimony:

> When you involve yourself, there is a connection . . . so people can deter-
> mine with time the mood of the cattle. The process of becoming friends
> doesn't need voice, and it doesn't need intellectual understanding. For
> example, I remember that we had milking cows, and if one of them was
> hungry, you can figure out that she won't be giving her milk. Or if she is
> acting out of sorts, from the very beginning, as you approach her, you can
> see that she is raising her ear, and glaring at you sideways, you immediately
> know that you should feed her. If not, she will retain her milk and you'll get
> nothing.

In various accounts, the phrase "Sabbath milk" was mentioned. While some described this milk as the calves' Sabbath treat, others delineated specific arrangements between Jews and non-Jewish neighbors.[18] These stipulated that any calf attempting to nurse on the Sabbath would be kept away from the cow owned by the Jews. Instead, Christians milked this cow on the Sabbath and used the milk. An informant from the Tigre region explained: "A Christian can take the Sabbath milk of a Jew's cow. If there's a Christian neighbor nearby, they let him take its milk. If there are little calves, they set them out in the field so that they don't use the milk. We aren't allowed to drink or sell Sabbath milk."

Sabbath milk was also described as the milk given to the Christians who looked after the calves on the Sabbath to make sure that they did not nurse from their mother: "You can't bring any milk out on the Sabbath, you mustn't touch [the milk]. The Christian will take it for himself. A guard watches the children of the cow so that they don't touch their mother and take her milk."

You know, the cow is not sacred in Ethiopia like in India.[19] Still, cows are very much liked. Very, very much. If you have a cow, you definitely get milk, at least for a certain period. You will not be hungry. If you have got injera or *qitta* [a kind of flat pan bread], sometimes you may not have enough items to prepare *watt* [stew]. You need to have onions, butter, and so on, even something for the fire. But if you have milk, a glass of milk can help you to immerse the qitta in it, to make it soft and take it. You get satisfied and at the same time milk has all the protein and the calcium and so on. So people have much respect for the cow. Even if the milk is not warm, if you make it into *ergo* [yogurt] it is still milk. In the old times and in remote places, if you go to someone's house, they do not give you water. No! No! They give you yogurt. If they don't have the hot-fresh milk, they give you yogurt, and people like it so much.

As a manifestation of this reality and these understandings, people were usually quite willing to lend out their milking cows to a sick relative or friend. The basis of this practice was the unquestioned conviction that the drinking of fresh milk was the best remedy for overcoming weakness and various diseases.

While collecting proverbs among Christians living in the area where the Beta Israel had lived, I heard a well-known proverb that portrays in Christian terminology the significance of the cow and her milk. The proverb was recited along with the following interpretation:

የሥጋ መድኃኒት ላም፤ የነፍስ መድኃኒት ማርያም
ye-siga medhanit lam; ye-nafs medhanit Maryam
Cow is medicine for the flesh; Mary is medicine for the soul

The explanation given to this proverbial analogy was that "just as the milk given to us by the cow cures us here on earth, so the Virgin Mary cures us in heaven. The cow and Saint Mary are both mothers," it continued, "and so here on earth it is the cow who gives milk and saves our children, and in heaven it is Mary who awaits to save us." These covenantal relations with the Holy Mother Mary, although obviously anchored in the teachings of the Ethiopian Orthodox Church, powerfully resonate within the Ethiopian general belief system and project on other mothers and other covenants, among them the practical and emotional relations with cows likely perceived as carrying sacred, covenantal dimensions.

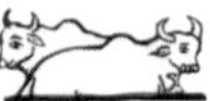

At this point it is illuminating to carefully listen to the story of the faithful cow "Lamie Bora" ("My Cow Bora"), which I repeatedly heard both in Israel and in Ethiopia. Although found in various versions, the story always displays a recognizable core. This can be the entire story or the first part of a story that expands in additional directions. Here is a pithy version which I heard in Israel:

Once upon a time there was a married couple with two small children, a girl and a boy. The mother became sick with a very serious illness. She began to worry very much about what might happen to her children if she were to die. Now, she had a cow that was called Bora, a name often given to an animal with a white patch on its forehead. In Ethiopia it is a common practice for people to call their animals with personal names, usually ones connected to the colors and markings on their skin. When the mother felt that she was near to death, she called for her beloved cow Bora that was always providing the family with abundant, high-quality milk. She turned to her cow and began to sing a special song to her: *"Lamie Bora, Lamie Bora, lijochan adera,"* which means: "My cow Bora, my cow Bora, my children are in your custody, [as an] *adera*"—a culturally specific concept that we shall explore. She continued to explain to her cow that she was very worried because she was afraid that after her death, her husband might take another wife who would neglect the two orphaned children. Therefore, she was pleading with her beloved cow to take care of them and make sure they would be raised properly. At the completion of her pleading song, the mother died.

Sure enough, soon after her death, the children's father found another woman for himself and married her. This woman had her own children, whom she preferred over the two children of her husband. She only worried about the needs of her own children. She didn't feed the orphans and was constantly neglecting them. Every day, the orphan children were very hungry as they went out to shepherd the cattle in the field. When they arrived in the field, they always sought out the cow Bora and sang to her: *"Lamie Bora, Lamie Bora, ateresh ye-enatachin adera."* This means: "My cow Bora, my cow Bora, don't forget our mother's adera." Immediately and right there, her udders filled up, enabling her to feed the children with all sorts of wondrous tastes that emerged from her milk. The two children would drink until they were satisfied. As a result, they turned into beautiful and well-nourished children. At the same time the stepmother's children, whom she fed herself, became ever skinnier no matter how much they ate.

The stepmother noticed all this, and decided to find out how this could be happening. One day she decided to follow the two children as they went out to the field, and thus she discovered that the cow Bora was feeding them. She returned home and spoke to her husband: "I don't feel well; I am sick. Slaughter for me this cow, so that after I eat from its meat, I will be healthy again." The husband did not know anything and did not understand. But the children heard all of this, and they quickly ran to Bora and told her. The cow listened and said: "Watch very carefully. When your father starts preparing the knife for slaughtering, run quickly to me and tell me." A few days later, early in the morning, the children heard their father sharpening his knife. Then they immediately ran to Bora and told her. The cow Bora did not hesitate. She hoisted the children up on her back and fled with them to the forest. There she raised them, caring for them until they matured, got married, and established their own households.[20]

While "Lamie Bora" is recognizably an international tale type,[21] in its particular cultural context it both establishes and expresses intimate sentiments held by the Ethiopian people in relation to their cows. The story depicts a sentimental drama dominated by three mothers: the biological mother, the stepmother, and the animal proxy mother—a beloved milk cow. Themes of loyalty and endless giving, as well as of reward and recompense, expressed by means of evocative words and melodies, are embedded in the story. These features not only serve as moral teachings, but they also provide an emotional compass. Altogether, the story both demonstrates and generates the covenantal mutual relations between humans and their precious, beloved cows.

These understandings and sentiments are amplified by means of the nexus with the concept of *adera*. While probing for the meaning of this term, central to the story of "Lamie Bora," I realized it was a revealing indigenous term, essential for an in-depth understanding of the Ethiopian cultural ethos. It was obviously difficult for my Ethiopian friends to translate the term, but after listening to many explanations, new dimensions of cultural significance became accessible.

Let us listen to Yitshak in Israel and to Ayalew in Ethiopia, who diligently sought to initiate me into the nuances of adera. Here is Yitshak:

Adera is very, very important. In Ethiopia, if you say adera, it is very obligating and the one to whom you said that cannot violate it. If you tell someone adera, he is committed to the word that came out of you. You will say it only to someone you trust, and in this way, you are in fact strengthening his commitment. The one who is being told adera will be highly motivated to whatever he was asked to fulfill. A person who doesn't follow adera, it is as if he forfeits his humanity. You just cannot refuse. It is even not under your authority or your right to refuse. For example, on our way to Israel via Sudan, one mother sent her daughter with one of us, saying *adera-hen*, and that person was obliged to protect her and take care of her.

Here is Ayalew:

> In the olden days and even today, when parents were near death and their children had nobody else to look after them, the dying parents will go to a respected person in the community—it could be a man or a woman—and simply ask them, or request them, or beg them that they look after their children. . . . This is the most important adera . . . and those people who accept adera, it is not even necessary for them to explain that they have accepted adera or not. Simply they are told to keep adera by the one who is dying. And all the people around, who heard the dying person giving adera, start to look after what that fellow is going to do. . . . The one who gives adera and the one who accepts it, they don't need witnesses. They only have to say that there is God between you and me. That's all. They do not write it down; it is all cultural. So strong, tight, so that they know that God will punish them if they break their adera. . . . Adera is keeping a word, a given word. Someone gives you his wishes, his feelings; he tells you, and you are going to guard those words—you will take them. And even if he is an enemy, when he says adera, then you will keep it; you will accept his words. . . . It is not a promise. It is not an oath—the one who is given adera, he may not even give a reply. He has to accept it. He doesn't ask any questions; he doesn't say anything. He simply accepts it.

Thus, adera is a constrictive obligation bound up in realms derived from a higher, divine authority that resonates even without any human agreement or approval. Despite its resemblance to the notion of a trust, adera is considered to be a sacred and binding transmission that does not require the expressed agreement of the receiver. At the moment adera is bestowed, it is incumbent on the receiver to carry it out. The community, with a critical eye, will closely observe the receiver's conduct to make sure adera is properly fulfilled. As a fundamentally abstract cultural concept, the meaning of adera is elusive and hard to convey, let alone explain. It is applicable to various actual contexts and situations as well as ideas and imaginations. One of them, the anguish of orphan children, which is central to the "Lamie Bora" story, provides an especially potent vehicle for this key concept and thus has tended to be its most frequently employed association.

In the story, Bora, the faithful cow, nourishes the children as part of adera that was bestowed on her by her owner, a dying mother. As the recipient of adera, the cow does not have to utter any sound or show any sign that she accepts it. Simply by her mute presence, the cow confirms her crucial role in this divine bestowal. The widespread diffusion of this story matches with the abiding centrality of the cow in everyday Ethiopian life. In my reading of the story, the unlimited giving of cows elevates them to the noble rank of ultimate adera conveyors for the entire Ethiopian people.

The very idea of slaughtering a milking cow is considered unthinkable. The stepmother's demand that Bora—the righteous cow that understood so well the power of adera—be slaughtered bespeaks a wretched act whose implementation is unbearable. The repulsion felt over the stepmother's demand is further accentuated because it is given precisely while the cow is devotedly fulfilling the command of adera.

As long as she is feeding the children, the cow cannot be slaughtered under any condition. Adera is understood to create a bond that is not amenable to being unraveled and is not dependent on the will of the one who receives it. Whoever cruelly severs adera is subverting not only binding social norms, but is also, so to speak, betraying God himself, under whose auspices adera is maintained.

In the Ethiopian perspective on the hierarchical relations between humans and animals and the inevitable loss inherent in their eventual slaughter, cows pose a riveting conceptual and sentimental challenge that calls for a suitable form of cultural resolution. The challenge is dealt with by way of this inspiring and touching folktale, and even more so by way of its crystallization around the powerful notion of adera. With this conjunction of Bora with adera, the pervasive reverence felt for the cow as an unlimited horn of plenty for human society is reinforced.

The following episode took place in the living room of an elderly couple in Israel. With moist eyes, my host, a vital eighty-year-old woman recalled that "every day she [the cow] was begging for salt. She very much loved salt. So we would mix barley with salt and feed her by hand. She loved it. Can you imagine such spoiling? I would roast the barley, mix it with salt, and serve it directly to her mouth. Also when I made *tella*, our delicious homemade beer, I would feed her the tasty dregs that had settled to the bottom of the jug. Whatever remained of the grains and fibers, she would eat. The cow would wait patiently to get this treat morning and night." At this point she mimicked the sounds that the cow made when waiting for these treats (see fig. 2.5). "Also, when my husband came back from work, the cow would chase after him until he gave her some fresh-cut green hay, which was her favorite." Now the husband, who is sitting with us, joins in to mimic the same cow's sounds of joy.

Their Ethiopian born daughter, sitting with us, intervenes to reflect on her parents' memories: "This feeding of their beloved cow caused them great satisfaction. The cows made them happy. A real feeling of happiness! Here in Israel the cows don't even smell good, but in Ethiopia it is something else. Also, Mother would tell us that because she was the youngest daughter in her family, she would always get to drink milk before anybody else, with all its foam, and she would drink it while it was still warm."[22]

In another testimony of closeness, I was told the story of a person whose cow cared for him to the extent of seeming to spoil him. Every day, on returning from work and after feeding his cow, he would bend his head in the cow's direction so that she could lick it with her rough tongue. Aside from being an enjoyable treat of closeness, this gesture was reported to have the benefit of removing lice. It's worth noting that the common practice of lice removal required close physical contact, and hence was generally carried out among family members. By performing this specific task, the cow seemingly insinuated herself as a member of the family.

The already mentioned practice of giving personal names to cattle was another expression of humans' affection for their livestock. Here too, the details of human-animal relations not only enable a nostalgic concreteness but are available as a means to reflect on present life in Israel. Some personal names were unique to cattle, while others could also be given to humans. I often heard about the ease with which the cows recognized their personal names, and in general, about their good manners: "If one of the cows would wander off somewhere and she hears her name called, she will return immediately. [In contrast] A sheep, no matter how much you talk to him, he is a tabula rasa, doesn't understand . . . here [in Israel] in the name of democracy everyone is spoiled; there is no order. In Ethiopia even the cows are well educated and disciplined."

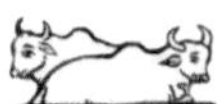

In rural Ethiopia, people were closely attuned to the health of their livestock and obliged to immediately treat them if any problem was discovered. This entailed a constant inspection of each animal's body and behavior. Health issues were therefore primary in the supervisory role of every livestock owner.

Figure 2.5. Bargaining over amole-chew (salt bars), Mekelle (Tigray), Ethiopia, 2015. Photo: Hagar Salamon.

Extensive knowledge concerning animal diseases was a crucial asset with significant economic ramifications. A failure to pinpoint even the smallest changes could quickly lead to catastrophic results for the individual animal and even the entire herd. In order to identify any potential problem, one had to be familiar with a wide range of physical symptoms as well as emotional signs. People described in detail how to identify healthy versus diseased animals, making it clear that the successful owner had to be something of a diagnostician, a psychologist, and a healer.

This in-depth knowledge served well when it came to purchasing animals in the weekly livestock market. Lengthy descriptions of the meticulous head to toe inspection that a person performed prior to purchase gave my interlocutors a chance to display their hard-earned expertise. People would describe vividly and with great pride how they conducted their examinations, starting with the color and shape of the teeth and extending to the condition of the webbing between the toes. No matter how vast and precise one's knowledge was, successful purchasing in the market remained a "matter of luck," I was told. There was always the danger of the seller having overly extolled the cow's milk potential or the ox's plowing capacity. If at all possible, the buyer looked for the opportunity to purchase from a friend or neighbor to check out the animal's performance in action, milking the cow himself or even taking the ox out to the field for a day's work.

As already noted, all mature male cattle are called berie, whether castrated or not, while a specified terminology subtly distinguishes between female cattle with regard to their place on a fertility continuum. These specifications, as mentioned before, include gider, the young cow not yet fertile; the fertile *lam*; the shehar, referring to a barren cow; and finally the *beltet*, an aged cow no longer able to give birth.

As the interviewees introduced these terms, it was clear that the hierarchy was based on fertility. Nevertheless, I also heard something else. It was precisely the barren shehar that captured the imagination of the speakers. People praised the shehar and excitedly described the unmatchable tastiness of her meat. Because she hadn't given birth, her flesh was believed to be fatter, softer, and tastier, and her price would be set accordingly. She was saved for the most special occasions and was served as an exceptionally relished delicacy.

Much attention was given to mating. When it was noticed that a cow was in heat, special blessings would be given by everyone to her owner. From that point onward, ever-present guarding was needed so that the preferred bull would be the one to impregnate her. As the cows were grazing in the open, the shepherds had to be on guard and chase away any uninvited bull whose genetic profile did not match the high standards looked for. During this period, an encounter had to be arranged between the ready cow and the chosen bull.

At this juncture, and in tandem with cattle-mating conventions, the story of the conception of Muchit, Mammit's younger sister, begs to be told. The following exposures include detailed descriptions of forced sexual encounters described by ex-slave barya women. In one of our many conversations, my friend Mammit shared her memories of the casualness of sexual episodes between choa and barya. The acts she described, which still haunt her, were apparently commonplace and acceptable in the context of traditional Ethiopian behaviors and understandings. One startling result of these engrained practices was the relatively frequent ignorance among the barya of their biological, rather than social, paternity. Knowing and lack of knowing as they correlate with strength and weakness, status as human and nonhuman, emerge in many areas, in which origin—both historical and personal—figures prominently.

The cynical use of the "power of knowing" is distilled in the story of the birth of Muchit.

Mammit casts a glance at her sister Muchit and said: "I want to tell you something. How Muchit was born—I'm going to tell you." The room fell silent, and everyone looked at Muchit. Mammit continued:

> Muchit's father is her [Sosana's] relation. He and his wife didn't have children. His wife's family said that he's the one who is barren, and not the woman, who was from their family. But his family said that it was actually she who was to blame, and not him. That's how they would argue. Then she [Sosana] said to him: "Go, grab her [Terengo]; get her pregnant, and prove to them that it's not you—it's them." That's just an example, get it? That's how it is; that's what he really did. That's how Muchit was born. "My slave woman is here, so come; come and do it to her." That's what she said to him. There wasn't anything that could be done. We are the ones he comes to rape, and then he rapes us. We can't do anything [about it]. Then afterwards, his wife, the one who was barren—he left her, and afterwards she died, and then he also had daughters from his second wife.

The story of Muchit's coming into being can be read as a trial in fertility. Terengo's body, on which the family's choa children were carried, is further being used as a means for supplying experimental knowledge about the fertility of the choa family. Witnessing this scene, my thoughts went back to the choa accounts. Their stories are replete with references to procreation, particularly the aggrandizing descriptions of their ability to preserve the inferior status of these offspring as barya and to assure that this mark be preserved for generations to come.[23]

The barya women who were raped described forced, brief contact. The "sex-grabber," as they called him, was often identified as a neighbor or member of the choa family compound. Some stories mentioned cases in which the grabber was an unknown passerby. Terengo, who slept in the open pen next to the cows (see fig. 2.6), was sexually vulnerable to every man. She could also be grabbed in the daytime while in the fields.[24] As narrated by Terengo and other ex-slave women, all this was a matter of social convention. The allowable, totally indifferent nature of "grab-sex" detached it from the realm of intimate relations while at the same time distancing it from the category of rape of a choa female, for which strict codes and sanctions are applied. Altogether, this complex of behaviors and related perceptions entirely ignores both the barya woman and the consequences of the act.

Figure 2.6. A booth for the cattle, Wolqait, Ethiopia, 2015. Photo: Hagar Salamon.

Despite this ingrained system, some barya women were occasionally forced into more exclusive sexual subjugation by choa men. These rare exceptions were always instigated by specific circumstances of the men involved. Given the sweeping and everyday nature of sexual abuse, these occurrences simply went unnoticed. Even if faint indications of sentiment were involved, these were reserved for the internal, taboo world of passion and fantasy intimately entwined with mastery and control. Moreover, barya women's accounts are characterized by restrained acceptance and despair-filled capitulation, including internalization of the cattle image: as a part of the family livestock, slave women were, in this setting, mute.[25] The fact that they began addressing the matter through speech only on their arrival in Israel emphasizes the totality of the internalization of the image that the choa chose for them and prompts a painful recasting of the choa's musing about the barya's likeness to cows: like a cow, who is mute, although it knows how to speak.

Notes

1. Amharic *qes* (plural *qessotch*) is used for both Beta Israel and Ethiopian Orthodox (Tewahedo) Church priests. With the move to Israel, the plural was Hebraized into *qessim*.

2. The word *barukh*, used frequently by the Beta Israel in response to prayers uttered by the priest, is used here to emphasize a mindless repetition, in the same way one might mindlessly answer "amen."

3. For a general discussion of choa perceptions regarding the barya and especially concepts of dehumanization, see Salamon (1994b, 75). In his paper on the history of slavery in Ethiopia, Fernyhough (2002), based on Tibebu (1995, 60), points out that slaves in Ethiopia were considered only partially human.

4. The topic of slavery among the Beta Israel unexpectedly emerged in the course of my fieldwork. On this phenomenon as a border marker between the Beta Israel and their Christian neighbors in Ethiopia, see Salamon (1994b, 72–88; 1999, 73–81). Regarding indications of past enslavement among Ethiopian Jews, see Flad (1869, 25) and Rapoport (1980, 19). On racial constructs and their folk narrative manifestations both in Ethiopia and Israel, see Salamon (2001 and especially 2003, 3–32). Past enslavement is still a sensitive issue in Ethiopia and for the older generation of the Israeli Ethiopian community. I have reflected on my position as an outsider probing on this submerged topic in the above-mentioned publications. More recently, however, I have witnessed an increased openness to raising and discussing the subject both in Israel and, more importantly, in Ethiopia. Two recent examples in which I personally participated include the special and expanded panel devoted to the subject in the last ICES (International Conference for Ethiopian Studies) held in Mekelle (Tigray, Ethiopia) in October 2018, in which speakers were both Ethiopian and foreign, as well as an entire issue of the established journal *Northeast African Studies* dedicated to slavery in Ethiopia (*Northeast African Studies* 17:2, 2017). Both are noteworthy and important indicators of a gradually changing attitude.

5. For the wider context of slavery among neighboring groups, see, for example, Griaule (1934–35); Messing (1962); Seifu (1972); Levine (1974); Derrick (1975); Pankhurst (1976); Leroy (1979); Fernyhough (2010); and especially McCann (1988).

6. On the use of the term *choa* in connection with educating young children to become well-mannered, see Rosen (1985, 56–57). On the use of the term historically in feudal Ethiopian society to refer to the nobility and military elites, see Crummey (1980, 121).

7. Although the term *barya* is considered related to a northern Ethiopian tribe of the same name from which slaves were taken in earlier periods, it has since acquired a wider association, implying an inferior slave status and racial origin not necessarily related to the original Barya tribe. On related racial dynamics among the Beta Israel, see Salamon (1994b; 1995; 2003).

8. On slavery and slave trade among other groups in the history of Ethiopia, see also Griaule (1934–35); Baravelli (1935); Messing (1957, 413–15; 1962, 386–408); Seifu (1972); Levine (1974, 56); Derrick (1975, 152); Pankhurst (1977); Leroy (1979);

Quirin (1997); Fernyhough (2002, 2010); Rapoport (1980, 19); Sawyer (1986, 220);
Abdussamad (1999).

9. In 1922, The League of Nations dealt with slavery in Ethiopia. The Ital-
ian invasion of Ethiopia was partly justified, Lovejoy and Hogendorn (1993,
362n106) mention, "on the basis that slavery was still widespread, and that its
suppression required formal occupation," as does Messing (1957, 413–32). On
the details of the rulings against the institution while still slavery was still practiced in Ethiopia between 1923 and 1942, see Derrick (1975, 153). On Ethiopia as
a Civilized Nation, slavery, and the League of Nations, see also Allain (2006).
Miers (2003, 303) reminds us that "the American Embassy reported in 1951 that
the sale of small children was 'commonplace' outside of Shawa and Tegre."
On enduring European efforts to eradicate slavery in Ethiopia, see Miers
(1991), and also 2003, where she concludes that slavery in Ethiopia has been
terminated.

10. Most prominent among these are the Noah stories both in the *Kebra Nagast*
(*The Glory of the Kings*, Ethiopian national epic) and the Old Testament (Genesis
21–23), associating the barya with Ham and the choa with Shem. These stories
provided over the generations a divinely approved explanation legitimizing master-
slave relations. On the myth of Shem and Ham and the image of the Black in Jewish
culture throughout history, see Melamed (2003, 53–59). On these stories as incorporated in the perceptions of the choa, see Salamon (1994b, 72–88; 2003, 3–32).

11. There is a vast literature regarding phenomena of shared conceptual frame-
works and images common to slaves and animals. For an overview, see Jacoby
(1994). On perceptions of barya otherness as expressed in interviews with Beta
Israel choa, see Salamon (1994b, 74–76).

12. See Salamon (2002; 2003).

13. To protect the anonymity of the interviewees, I use fictional names. A few
interviewees, however, asked to appear with their real names.

14. The title Abba, meaning "father," denotes respectability and honor and was
often attached to a master's name by ex-slave interviewees.

15. At this point it is worth reminding the reader that drinking blood is not
practiced in highland Ethiopia, although Christians eat raw meat, as described
elsewhere in this book.

16. Known in Amharic as *qibe*, butter has been prized for having both healing and beautifying properties. Among its many uses, women put it regularly on
their hair as well as in the mouth of a newborn baby so as to keep his voice from
becoming harsh (see Levine 1965, 220). Among Oromo groups, such as the Tulama
of Shewa, butter is used in *gadaa* ceremonies to anoint ritualistic trees (see, for
example, Nicolas 2006, 171).

17. This reminds us of the biblical story regarding the nursing of Moses: "Then his sister asked Pharaoh's daughter, 'Shall I go and get one of the Hebrew women to nurse the baby for you?'" (Exodus 2:7, New International Version). The fact that Mammit's mother was religiously part of the Beta Israel is significant to the story.

18. A well-known ancient Jewish tale, reflecting intimacy between cows and their human owners, tells of a cow whose Jewish owner was obliged to sell it to a Gentile to pay his debts. The cow, accustomed to resting on the Sabbath, continued to do so in its new home. The new owner threatened to take back his money, so the Jew approached the cow's ear and gently whispered his plight. The cow did as asked. The Gentile was so impressed that he converted to Judaism . . . (Midrash Decalogue, the fourth commandment). I thank Galit Hasan-Rokem for this reference. Milking on Sabbath and even the option to let a non-Jew do so has long been an issue of Halakhic debates. Interestingly, this issue, for which an acceptable solution was practiced by the Beta Israel, was a matter of Jewish controversy and Zionist history, especially around milking on Sabbath by non-Jews in kibbutzim.

19. This comparison between sacredness of the cow in Ethiopia and India recalls the seminal work of Marvin Harris (1987) on the history of the sacredness of the cow in India.

20. As already mentioned, the story "Lamie Bora" has manifold versions. To add only one short example, a popular version relates how the stepmother climbed a rock to watch the slaughter of Bora. In her haste she slipped and fell then and there to her death. According to my Ethiopian friend Ayalew, who told me the story, he heard this version as a child in Sunday school.

21. Branching from the Cinderella tale type, it can be categorized according to the folkloristics index of tale types as Aarne and Thompson (1973) AT tale type 510. For a highly relevant study on Cinderella and cows, see Vas da Silva (2014).

22. This has even more significance as the conventional practice is to feed adults before children and offer elders the choicest food. For reflections on the Ethiopian custom of feeding a person sitting at one's table by placing a handful of sumptuous food in his or her mouth, known in Amharic as *gursha*, see Salamon (2019).

23. For a detailed discussion of the linguistic and conceptual terms applied to the children of such a union, as well as the fastidious preservation of genealogical knowledge among the choa, see Pankhurst (1976, particularly 17, 30–31), and see Salamon (1994b, 58–72) on slavery and the genealogical memory of the Beta Israel.

24. When she uses the Hebrew root t-f-s (to grab, catch), she is referring to intercourse in its physical sense but also intimating, at least rhetorically, at the possibility of her still breaking away and escaping his clutch.

25. The reverse comparison arises in descriptions of slavery in other cultural contexts, including the stories of Toni Morrison who, for example, in *Beloved*, mentions in passing, as if obvious, the existence of sexual contacts of slaves with cattle (Morrison 1987, 10–11). In the descriptions at the center of the present work, it is human sexual relationships that come across as bestiality.

Zooming Out

Emerging from the Pen

Moving out from close-up shots of the intimate, hierarchical human relations leading to reproduction, we now go to the happy moments surrounding the birth of a calf. If everything went as planned and the cow safely delivered her healthy offspring after nine months, it called for a local celebration. Neighbors would be invited, coffee and special injera prepared, and blessings for health and future procreation exchanged. But the highlight of the party was a milking ceremony. The new mother's early milk was highly esteemed and believed to have special healing properties, not just for the newborn calf but also for humans. Family and close neighbors were eager to share the warm liquid and enjoy its benefits. Overall, this postbirth party was taken as a source of present and future prosperity.

The basis of a new family herd came with the dowries (*macha*) agreed on by the families of a young couple. The macha usually included a young cow for her and a young bull for him. Some families were rich enough to give more than a single animal, while others could not afford any. Nevertheless, the standard practice was set up so that the newly married couple would have a cattle couple, so to speak, accompanying them from the start of their marital relationship, as expressed in the declaration "with this you begin your life." In addition to the living animals, the young couple would be presented with an expertly treated hide, taken from a mature cow, to serve as bedding in their new home. The cattle and especially the cow had a central place in the expected prosperity of the couple both economically and symbolically.

Shifting the focus once again to slavery, I was told with great pride by choa interviewees that barya and their offspring were passed on, just like cattle, from one generation to the next as part of the macha: "Back then, my grandmother bought a barya with money. . . . After some time, she [the barya] had children, and then the barya's children were given by my grandmother as macha. Like a cow, they also give barya if they have children; they give the barya like they give a cow."

Obviously, gender-related tasks of both wife and husband were reinforced by the gender of the given animal, so that "his" bull would help in the fields while "her" cow provided the household with milk and calves. Moreover, the very fact that the animal couple was introduced simultaneously with the married couple suggested an ever-present shadow family, whose welfare was inevitably intertwined with that of the new couple. The kernel of this idea can be seen in the following elaborate and insightful descriptions. While speaking with an elderly woman about the early stage of her marriage and birth giving, she exclaimed, "Me and my cow every two years! Not exactly at the same precise time, but we both gave birth every two years. You can see that she is in heat when all the bulls come chasing her. The pregnancy of the cow is nine months, just like ours. You can see by her belly and also her breasts [that she is pregnant]. Just like with a woman." It is worth noting that it was customary for the husband's family to give an additional calf (or sometimes a bull or cow) to the young mother, in honor of the newly born baby.

Relating to his own wedding, a male interviewee explained that "when we got married, my wife received a cow, and I got a bull. . . . Now, once you have with you this couple—a cow and a bull—and you feed them well and give them all they need, she can suddenly become pregnant. This is like what happens with people, the woman who is well taken care of begins to preen herself and will soon become pregnant."

These illuminating equations not only contribute to our appreciation of the economic aspects of marriage in rural Ethiopia but reveal another facet of the deep sentiments felt for cattle and especially cows. With all these sentiments in mind, it is clear that to take a cow to slaughter and prepare her flesh to be eaten are emotionally highly charged acts. The next section opens with a selfie, a firsthand account taken at a Christian repast in Ethiopia, illustrating from a markedly different perspective the multifaceted nature of those sentiments.

Figure 3.1. Wednesday evening: A healthy ox has been tied to the pole in front of the restaurant, January 2015. Photo: Hagar Salamon.

In January 2015, my spouse Amos and I traveled from Israel to rural Northwest Ethiopia. It was shortly after *Timqat*, the Ethiopian Orthodox celebration of Epiphany, which falls in the dry season. This time of the year is a festive period, a time for weddings as well as church-related gatherings, all marked by a surfeit of meat consumption. On our way to a Saint Mary's church celebration and accompanied by an Ethiopian friend, we looked for a place to eat in a small town south of Bahir-Dar. Our friend suggested that we have our meal at a popular local restaurant. Approaching the place, we found ourselves face-to-face with a huge, impressive ox, tied to a wooden post, standing mildly at the entrance to the restaurant, forcing us to skirt around him to enter (see fig. 3.1). Inside, there were many low tables but very few customers. We looked at each other with some suspicion, concerned that it might be a wrong choice. Indeed, the owner could offer only a very limited menu based on *shero* (a traditional chickpea dish), pasta, and some vegetables. At that point our Ethiopian friend reminded us that it was a Wednesday and therefore the menu was bound to be limited, since in Christian Ethiopia all animal derived dishes are prohibited. Meat, eggs, and milk products are excluded on the two weekly fasting days: Wednesdays and Fridays. Besides these two days, there are several extended annual fasting periods when no meat or related animal products are allowed.[1] So that evening

Figure 3.2. Thursday morning: Preparation of the ox at the restaurant. Photo: Hagar Salamon.

we made do with a vegetarian pasta meal. Leaving the restaurant to spend the night in a nearby hotel, we saw that the ox was still standing there impassively.

The next morning, again accompanied by our Ethiopian friend, we passed the same restaurant and couldn't believe the bustle. The atmosphere was elevated. This time, unlike the previous evening, all tables were full, and dozens of diners were heartily devouring meat. To our astonishment, we were faced with the now-bloody body of the ox, attached to a slatted white wooden frame as if on display for the appreciation of the many enthusiastic participants to the consumption of its flesh. Standing in front of the deceased ox were two butchers attired in all white gowns and high white chef's caps (see fig. 3.2). They were continuously and nimbly carving off small chunks of meat, which they weighed out in portions according to each person's request. Some asked for their portions to be cooked, but most ate them raw with great gusto, accompanied by *berberrie,* hot red chili pepper paste. Except for the standard injera and the

Figure 3.3. Thursday morning: The ox's hide now placed in front of the restaurant. Photo: Hagar Salamon.

ever-welcome beer, the repast was all about meat. In front of everybody's eyes, the ox was quickly dissolving into a bare carcass. Mesmerized by the spectacle, I was totally taken with the unequivocal relevance of this event to the topics with which I was dealing. The next few hours provided a firsthand encounter that no words had ever conveyed regarding the sensational and emotional elements attached to the Ethiopian craving for meat. The total immersion of all participants in the feast was captivating.

When we finally left the restaurant, we noticed a wrapped bundle that had been placed just a few steps away from the post where the live ox had stood the day before (see fig. 3.3). On closer inspection, it turned out to be the skin that had covered the living body of that very same ox. Clearly, it had been deliberately placed there for inspection by anyone entering the restaurant. My friend proudly explained that it was proof to any concerned customer that the meat being served inside was that of the exact ox that had been on display the day before. He pointed out that this maintained the reputation of the restaurant. The local passersby had quite likely formed their impression of the tastiness of the early morning slaughter of that ox and their appetites were already whetted in anticipation of the upcoming feast. When they saw the actual skin, they could be confident that yesterday's flesh is today's meat.

Further reflecting on the entire scene, I realized the deep internalization of the strict regimen of weekly and yearly meat permissions and prohibitions for the local population. Although the entire scene took place in a restaurant, the meat was prepared by two meat carvers in Western attire, and what we witnessed was totally Christian, it is in this cultural context and in tandem with such highly charged carnivorous sentiments that the Beta Israel's own practices and attitudes regarding meat were shaped.

The overpowering sentiments that encompass the scene described above characterize other meat-eating occasions I witnessed and heard about in Israel. In rural Ethiopia, it is often an ox that has worked for years alongside its owner in the field or a cow that has long been attached to the family that is now being served as a tasty dish. This inevitable transformation is obviously fraught with anguish and requires an enabling cultural framework. The framework is primarily constructed by means of the religious commandments of both Christians and Jews. It is powerfully manifested in holidays, life cycle celebrations, and especially the well-established weekly and yearly fasting regimes.[2] With the insights engendered by this encounter, we now turn back to an elaboration of the Beta Israel conceptions of meat eating.

To better appreciate what it meant to eat meat, one has to look at the Beta Israel's overall cuisine. Their daily diet was grain based, including wheat, barley, sorghum, and *teff*, an indigenous grain-like seed popular throughout Ethiopia. Teff and barley were used for the preparation of a type of flatbread called *injera*. Injera was served with a variety of stews (*watts*) mostly made of lentils, chickpeas, and local vegetables and spiced with hot pepper (berberrie) and a variety of other condiments. This meal was usually eaten communally, with numerous diners sitting around a table-like tray. Each person would take a piece of the injera and dip it into various stews. In addition, the Beta Israel enjoyed native-grown coffee (*bunna*), which was roasted, ground, and savored during an elaborate and beloved coffee ceremony. Additional favorite drinks in that region included *tella*—a homemade beer prepared from a mixture of barley, hops, local herbs, and water—and the honey wine or mead known as *tejj*. Thus, traditional eating customs emphasized commensality and sharing among the participants in the meal.

In contrast to the simplicity of this everyday, basically vegetarian menu, meat eating stood out for its festiveness. The most frequently eaten meat was chicken, followed by goat and sheep, with cattle being rarely consumed.[3] Chicken might be eaten even on a weekly basis, usually on Sabbath; goat was typically prepared for important guests; and sheep was connected with certain holiday celebrations, the most prominent being Passover (*Fasika*), during which male sheep were sacrificed and consumed.[4] Cattle meat consumption was reserved for annual-cycle and life cycle celebrations. Only such major events merited the sacrifice of cattle. This deep-rooted hierarchy regarding meat was of course reinforced by practical exigencies.[5]

A complex range of considerations, rules, and regulations lent priority to consuming male cattle. In comparison with the cow, the ox was fat enough, and consuming its meat was considered a source of special strength. Young calves were kept safe and exempt from slaughter until they reached a certain age. Years after moving from Ethiopia to Israel, men still had a vivid, tactile image of measuring the size of a calf's horns to determine its age and permissibility for consumption in rare cases of family distress.[6]

The underlying conceptual framework related to slaughter constitutes a central axis in the understanding of human relations and beyond. The more the animal had been a partner, and the deeper the owner's feelings toward it, the more its slaughter and consumption became both weighty and festive.[7]

From among the cows, the fertile ones were seldom if ever eaten. Moving to the infertile cows, the meat of a young barren cow (shehar) was considered, as mentioned, especially desirable. Recollections of her meat seemed to arouse enthusiasm over and above that of any other animal. In contrast, the meat of a postfertile cow was looked at equivocally. I was repeatedly told how difficult it was to even consider eating the meat of a postfertile cow. This split may be due, of course, to the differences in the sheer quality and taste of the meat. But it seems that there was much more to it. The cow that had brought so much to the family over many years stimulated sentiments and complexities related to the cow's maternal role. It was as if motherhood made her flesh especially difficult to digest.[8] To come to terms with this reticence, people might try to sell such a cow to somebody who had no special feelings for her. This compassion is well expressed in the following account: "Because they were yours for so many years, you become attached to them. He gave you the fullest extent of his economic potential, and she gave you the milk and her births. So now at the end to slaughter them? No! Better to sell yours and buy from someone else for slaughtering."

These uneasy sentiments raised by the eating of an old cow, so long a highly valued contributor to the family, brought to my mind the scandalous story of Twawosh, known as Grandma, and the attempt to sell her. She was the property of Abba Legesse's wife, Sosana, since Twawosh's mother had arrived as part of Sosana's macha when she married Abba Legesse.

The barya women, when recalling the story of selling Grandma, recount that it was Tedesa (son of Abba Legesse and Sosana) who came up with the idea to sell her.[9] He lured her into accompanying him on a journey from which she did not return until many years later. Once they were outside the village, he took her hostage and sold her to slave traders: "At night, they left Grandma Twawosh in the field, tied her hands, and they also tied thorns to her feet with string—it is known that in Ethiopia when they don't want someone or even an animal to run away, they tie thorns to their feet. They also put a piece of cloth in her mouth so that she wouldn't scream."

They then went from house to house trying to sell her, claiming she had strong teeth, was a good worker, and could bear children. Twawosh managed to intervene, divulging that she was no longer menstruating: "Luckily, the man [who bought her], who was also very rich, was impressed with her qualities and said to her: 'You're a good woman who tells the truth. . . . My wife is about to give birth, so we'll need help, and I'll buy you.' And he bought her from them, and he even gave her a cow and said to her: 'Because you told me the truth, I'm giving you a cow, so that you'll have your own cow.'"

Grandma worked for this Christian family for about five years until she was bought back by Tedesa, who couldn't bear the rage of his father and neighbors: "Everyone said to him 'How could you sell your mother?[10] You sold a good woman who raised you and carried you on her back when you were children, gave you food—why don't you sell your own children?'"

Once Tedesa eventually located Twawosh's whereabouts, he had to pay back twice what he had been paid for her.

> He sold a lot of cows for her. It took time to get the money together . . . and now what? That goy [gentile, Christian] she worked for wanted to give her a cow that she would take with her. That's a lot of money. But what did Twawosh say? "Keep the cow for yourself. Thank you very much just for letting me go. Thank you very much for freeing me and letting me go to my children," and she kissed his foot and all that, and as for the cow, she said to him "It's from me, I'm leaving it for you. Just bless me and pray that I get to my children in peace, and the cow—it will be a present for you." She didn't want to take the cow. Look, it's far. You can't take a cow so far. "Just bless me"—that's important. Do you see Twawosh, how good she is?

Cows emerge at many points in this story as the leitmotif connecting it with reality; it is as though the image of the cow stirs up feelings more powerful than those evoked by merely describing human relations. Grandma, portrayed as the one who carried all the family's children on her back, had been abducted, her innocence and trust in the family betrayed. Each narrator took pride in Grandma's courage to speak up, if only to attest to her inability to bear children. Grandma is similarly admired for her refusal to accept the cow given to her by her new owner. Years later, this new owner's demand for steep payment for her return is also transposed to the cows that must be sold to redeem her. The description of Grandma's grandeur culminates in her relinquishing of the cow offered to her on returning to the family compound. With this, the humanity of she who had been sold like a cow receives a mark of distinction. A transition occurs from the choa's statements about the barya being inferior to cows, since their blood cannot be drunk nor their flesh consumed, to the description of Grandma on whose behalf cows are sold, and who herself declined to accept the cow offered to her.

Looking further into the turmoil over eating one's own faithful cow, one finds nuanced attitudes. While most people expressed reticence, some stressed that it is perfectly fine to eat one's own beloved cow, as long as the meat is religiously permissible. According to these individuals, the important thing is to comply exactly with divine commandments, and in so doing give honor to the animal they love so much. Being consumed following a meticulous religious procedure elevates the animal, as it fulfills to completion the role bestowed on it. A further reinforcement of this perception comes from the holy contexts in which meat is prescribed. These two approaches are well summed up in the following statement, given to me as a reply to my question regarding slaughter for a family wedding: "Some people would take it [the cow] from their own house, and there are those who say that they can't. But there is no exact halacha [religious law] about what is correct. There are those who just don't feel comfortable and sell their cow, and there are those who use their own and say, 'This is the use, and that is the way of the world.'"

The following zoomed-in account from Mammit can be interjected into the above wide-angle framework: "Another thing Sosana did to us, besides beating us, was to bite us—she felt like that, just like that, so she would bite us hard on the hands and face. Abba Legesse would beat us. He would beat us with a stick, but he wouldn't bite. Sosana would bite. She would bite us when we were at home, not outside—not in front of people. Our hands, our cheeks, our legs—we had marks everywhere. To this day we have scars from her bites."

Sosana's vicious, ongoing bites occurred in the context of a vocabulary replete with cannibalistic images, which she often employed. Thus, her biting may be seen as attempts to taste the barya's inedible flesh. With its repeated explicit denials—an example of which is cited below—this episode testifies to Sosana's deep ambivalence toward the barya women, whom she perceived as beings located somewhere along the continuum between human and cows. Her manifest cannibalistic tendencies direct attention to the very impossibility of carrying them out to completion. Recalling her mother's and aunt's pregnancies and births, as well as her grandmother's many miscarriages, Mammit told me that "they think they are God. That they are *like* God. They don't care at all. That evil Sosana would always say to us, 'What will I do with you? What? Will I drink your blood? What will I do with you? What, will I eat you, like cows? Because there are a lot of you—what do I need you for?' It was as if our family was too big. But she lived on our strength."

Most of all, due to the limited means of food preservation, the slaughter, preparation, and consumption of cattle had to be carried out to feed people on the spot, usually in large gatherings. Meat was cut into small chunks for immediate consumption or dried, usually by hanging elongated strips of raw meat (*qwanta*) above a smoking hearth (see fig. 3.4). Most commonly, meat was served to guests at weddings, funerals, or memorial services (*tazkar*) performed at specific intervals to enable the soul of the deceased to reach heaven. In other cases, the cattle meat could be divided among a large number of families, usually on the occasion of a major holiday (see fig. 3.5). Women took care of all daily meals, and in general men did not involve themselves in cooking. Nevertheless, when it came to animal slaughter and the preparation of the meat for cooking, women were excluded. These tasks were reserved for men.

An edifice of belief marks the transformation from the living to the edible as pivotal and indisputably under the hegemony of males.[11] In accordance with its ritual-religious nature, slaughter was done publicly and according to strictly observed religious rules. Among the Beta Israel, those charged first and foremost with animal slaughter were the priests, followed by married men who were familiar with the laws of ritual slaughter. Following these male-dominated, highly charged initial stages in treating the meat, women took over to cook the savory stews (see fig. 3.6).

Figure 3.4. Strips of meat (qwanta) above a smoking hearth, Bahir Dar vicinity, 2017. Photo: Hagar Salamon.

Figure 3.5. Cooperative preparation of meat to be served in an upcoming wedding, Addis Zeman, 2017. Photo: Hagar Salamon.

Figure 3.6. A pot of meat to be served in an upcoming wedding, Addis Zeman, 2017. Photo: Hagar Salamon.

In December 1984, a memorial ceremony for a very prominent Beta Israel qes was held in Ashdod, Israel.[12] Due to the deceased's eminence, his tazkar drew hundreds of people from both within and outside of the community, all of whom squeezed into his daughter's tiny two-room apartment. One of the attendees, an outsider to the community with whom I spoke years later, retained vivid memories of the occasion.[13] In describing the scene, he recalled his astonishment over the omnipresence of meat: blood was splattered around the entrance to the apartment building, suggesting a recent slaughtering of animals. Apparently, this slaughtering happened in the open courtyard at the back of the building. Pots were being filled with raw meat, and volunteers from the community were carrying them upstairs to the third-floor apartment. Fresh sheepskins were hanging over the banisters of the staircase. Inside the apartment, pieces of bloody meat were strung up on a rope over the bathtub, and pots full of cut-up raw meat were stored in the tub. From there, pots of meat were periodically carried to the tiny kitchen to be prepared as stew to serve the many guests who had come in honor of the tazkar. These practices, gradually modified, were liable to lead to clashes with non-Ethiopian neighbors, who often were offended or even repelled by the totally alien mourning customs being performed in the public space.

The particulars of this event dovetail with another episode that involved my close friend, the late Qes Avraham. After a few years in Israel, he took on a heavy financial burden by leaving his low-rent apartment and purchasing a private house. At that time, with the rapid growth of the Ethiopian Jewish community in Israel, attending life cycle ceremonies had become an ever-expanding commitment. These ceremonies invariably involved feeding guests with meat. This required purchasing an animal, slaughtering it, and cooking it—all by members of the then newly arrived community. Scenes like the gory one described above became more commonplace in neighborhoods inhabited by Ethiopian newcomers.

Looking back, I believe that these rather frequent conflicts motivated Qes Avraham's efforts to find a solution. Abandoning the slaughtering was not an option for him. This procedure was obviously an inviolable materialization of his religious standing and communal authority. He was determined to move from the apartment building where he lived to a private house with an enclosed courtyard. When I asked him about this unusual decision, he asserted that he needed his own place for slaughtering, both for himself and his community. My first visit to his new house along with my spouse was a special occasion for which Qes Avraham and his gracious wife roasted a goat. Serving us the meat, he proudly told us that he had just slaughtered the goat in his own backyard. As we shared together the flavors of the fresh goat, his decision to move to a private house became tangible. I realized that maintaining steadfast control over traditional meat-related procedures was a crucial feature in his expanding identity.

Occasionally, livestock would die accidently. In these cases, it was forbidden for the Beta Israel to consume the meat of the departed, unslaughtered animal. The owner could attempt to sell it to his non-Jewish neighbors, knowing that he would have to compromise on the price, or else just feed it to the dogs. In such cases, just as in regular slaughtering, the animals still had much to offer: hides, horns, hooves, and other very specific organs. As to the hide, great care was taken to remove it in its entirety. This required special skills: removing the

Figure 3.7. Leather thongs under a hide, Gondar market, 2015. Photo: Hagar Salamon.

skin of a sheep or a goat without damaging it was a common test that a groom was expected to pass prior to his wedding.

As mentioned earlier, the skin would be immersed in cattle urine, found to be effective in removing the blemishes and hair (see fig. 2.3). In the next stage, the skin would be treated by means of either animal fat or preferably bone marrow extracted from the animal's leg bones. Indeed, we see that the cattle not only provided their skin, but also the means by which it became beneficial to their owners. The high regard for a complete, processed cattle skin is linked with its use as bedding. As already mentioned, as part of her macha the bride is expected to bring to her new home a whole, unused hide (*genedi*), usually dyed red. This skin becomes softer over the years, thus indicating the successful marriage.

Uses for the hides were multiple and included specialized sacks with which to gather produce in the fields, decorated back carriers for babies, and cut strips to be used in a wide variety of daily and ritualistic activities (see fig. 3.7, 3.8, and 3.9).

Cattle horns were not discarded and instead were to make a variety of vessels. The most popular of these were small cups, spoons, and special honey

Figure 3.8. Decorated leather baby carriers, Gondar and Bahir Dar vicinities, 2015. Photo: Hagar Salamon.

Figure 3.9. Decorated leather baby carriers, Gondar and Bahir Dar vicinities, 2015. Photo: Hagar Salamon.

wine (tejj) containers. The hooves were cooked, split open, and the soft carti-
lage removed so that it could be added to a stew. The arteries and veins which
were, in the words of one of the interviewees "not bone, nor meat, nor fat and
therefore forbidden to eat," were thoroughly dried. They were then made into
threads used for sewing heavy fabrics including leather. As already mentioned,
a special function was reserved for the penile skin of oxen and bulls. After the
organ was dried, the round skin, known to be strong and flexible, was processed
and became an essential part in the making of the cattle whip. This kind of
whip was cherished for the characteristic sound it made, which stimulated the
working oxen to do their utmost (see fig. 2.2). As mentioned above, the bulls'
testicles, like those of other uncastrated livestock, also merited a special use.
They were cooked separately and served to male adolescents, passing on their
procreative potential.

Notes

1. On fasting etiquette of the Ethiopian Orthodox Church, see, for example,
Isaac (1995) and Zellelew (2014).

2. Compare this to the poem of a Gojjami farmer cited by Getie Gelaye: "Bring
me my oxen, let me slaughter and eat them/Before they [local administrator or
committee members] cut them into pieces like they did with my farmland"
(Gelaye 1999, 139).

3. Pork was not eaten by the Beta Israel, nor by their Muslim or Christian neighbors. The Christian Ethiopian prohibition on eating pork is related to the biblical
nature of Ethiopian Christianity. On this, see Ullendorff (1968) as well as Levine
(1974, 53).

4. As many of the interviewees noted, male sheep and goats (both known as
moket) had the sole purpose of providing meat. To better fulfill their mission, they
were castrated at the age of about one year so that their bodies would be fuller.

5. Attempts to understand sacrificial rituals have long held a prominent place
in the ethnography of religions. See Firth (1963) and more recently Reed (2013)
for anthropological notions and practices of sacrifice and offering. For a comprehensive collection of core articles on sacrifice, as well as an enlightening general
introduction, I refer the reader to Carter (2003). For an early and detailed description of Jewish sacrificial practices (including early notes on Falasha practices), see
"Sacrifice (Jewish)" in Hastings's *Encyclopedia of Religion and Ethics* (1924 (xi):
24–29).

6. As already described in the text, a nuanced terminology existed to depict the
many stages of calf development from birth (embosa), through suckling (qeja), to
grass eating (weifen for the male and gider for the female), and finally to a mature,
edible young animal (lam or berie).

7. For a structural, ideological approach regarding the consumption of different animals in American culture, see Sahlins (1976).

8. In regard to these mother-related sentiments, I refer the reader to Kristeva's *Powers of Horror* (1982).

9. The reasons for this decision are unclear to the tellers of the story, and during the many interviews and the constant retelling of the act of sale, various speculations that lay beyond the framework of the present book were raised. When Grandmother was sold, slave trading had been already outlawed in Ethiopia. Still, the bitterness inherent in the story is related to the thanklessness expressed by this specific sale rather than to the very idea of selling human beings and treating them as property.

10. On the tension between family ties and property, see Hoskins (2004). This tension is particularly striking in the accusation voiced at Tedesa: "You sold your mother." This, of course, echoes the folktale "Lamie Bora" discussed earlier.

11. For a feminist perspective on the similarity between objectifying food animals and objectifying women, see the works of Adams (1990, 1992, and especially 2004).

12. This ceremony took place in the midst of Operation Moses, the secret and dramatic operation by which thousands of Beta Israel members left Ethiopia to Israel via Sudan. For more on this operation, see introduction and related notes 10 and 11 in that chapter.

13. I thank my colleague and friend Dr. Chaim Rosen for this recollection. It was the tazkar of Qes Birhan Baruk, who had been one of the foremost traditional Ethiopian religious leaders actively working for Aliyah to Israel. As acknowledgment for his decades-long efforts, he and his family were among the first to be taken out of Wallega, near Gondar, a few years prior to Operation Moses. At the time it was hoped that he would also be active in Israel as a mediator between the rabbinate and the anticipated wave of newcomers. Rosen recalls that among those attending the tazkar were the Chief Rabbi of Ashdod, all of the other qessim already in Israel at the time, and many Aliyah activists and academics who had met him on their visits to Gondar.

Shifting Lenses

Interreligious Negotiations

In almost all everyday dealings with their livestock, Jews' behavior was similar to their Christian and Muslim neighbors, as human-animal relations were relatively unaffected by religious differences. Thus, it can be said that living animals had an equalizing potential that stood in contrast to the discrimination prevailing in almost every other area in the life of the Jews as a minority in Ethiopia. Relations with living animals were unsullied by oppressive social attitudes and generated sentiments of self-worth and dignity. The cows of the Jews and those of their neighbors were equally assessed and evaluated. No cow was inferior or superior due to her owner. Most likely, this has contributed to the fact that the Jews, even years later, gaze back on their animals and see them surrounded by a singularly untainted aura. However, at the critical moment of slaughter, the very same animal could be said to serve as a nexus of difference, carrying the complex relations between the different religious groups living side by side.

It was the actual body of the animal that conveyed the critical dynamics of discernment, among them those of sameness and difference: animals that had been a model of equality when alive became markers of strict separation when slaughtered. Indeed, slaughtering and meat eating figure prominently in the separation between Jews and Christians in Ethiopia.[1] In fact, meat cemented the Beta Israel's Jewish identity. Along with accounts relating to mutual beliefs, minute depictions of the prevailing slaughtering practices and meat-eating customs of each group were constantly raised, ever intensely loaded and emotionally charged.

Only in a few villages was the population made up exclusively of Beta Israel. In most cases, the Jews lived in mixed villages along with Christians, Muslims, or, in some instances, polytheists. Even though they were indistinguishable both physically and linguistically from their Christian neighbors, it was with Christians that relations were most complex.

An elaborate system of daily contacts existed between Jews and Christians, formalities of attraction and repulsion, which permitted structured cooperation but at the same time set strict boundaries between the groups. Working primarily in agriculture, most of the Beta Israel farmers were tenants on lands leased from Christians.[2] Ties between Christian landowners and Jewish tenants were based on various types of mutual agreements, most of which involved the tenants giving the owner a certain percentage of their crop each year as payment on the lease. The link also facilitated reciprocal help in the field—working together on the same plot, particularly during the planting and harvest seasons. During these seasons, Jews and Christians spent a great deal of time together working, eating, and talking.

The Beta Israel negotiated their Jewish identity by interacting with narratives, customs, and beliefs of the dominant Christian population. Discussing these topics in our interviews, I recognized embedded themes that called to mind the classic oedipal drama between Judaism and Christianity.[3] Their stories were a narrative template of a new, more youthful religion born from and yet dominating an older "father" religion. The drama was powerfully reenacted in the ironic inversions of daily interactions characteristic of life in rural Ethiopia.

Prior to mass immigration to Israel, the relations between the Beta Israel and their non-Jewish neighbors contained elements of stark repulsion softened by means of interactions indicative of mutual respect and attraction. On the one hand, the Beta Israel spoke of a chaotic atmosphere of fear and intimidation, in which they faced blood libel accusations, widespread dehumanizing beliefs, and omnipresent physical attacks. Concurrently, they described an alternative, more serene reality based on cooperation, easygoing conviviality, and even commonplace, dependable friendships between Christians and Jews. The palpable ambivalence of the relations is discernible in an array of indigenous beliefs and frequently observable customs. To varying degrees, these illustrate repulsion, attraction, or a combination of the two.

To supplement their family income, Beta Israel men would work as black-smiths, while the women specialized in pottery making. The dominant Christian population considered all manual occupations as tainted and looked at manual workers with distain. Nonetheless, they appreciated the excellence of Beta Israel products, which included indispensable items such as plows, knives, and weapons, along with pots and household utensils. Since these specific products require the application of fire to transform materials, the Beta Israel were both esteemed and feared. Their manual dexterity was considered an indication of an intimate association with supernatural powers, in particular the *buda*, the mythical hyena that figures prominently in Ethiopian cosmology.[4] Specifically, the Christians believe that the buda is able to disguise itself as human during the day, only to revert to its natural hyena state at night.[5] Whereas the belief in human/animal transformations appears in regard to other groups of similar craftworkers in Ethiopia (and elsewhere in Africa),[6] the concrete accusations linking the buda and the Beta Israel have certain unique features. These accusations encompass both their professions as artisans and their religious traditions.

The belief in the powers of the buda exposes a viewpoint predicated on the total dehumanization of the Jews. Considered to be essentially "hyena people," the Beta Israel induced fear in their neighbors. They were believed to have an insatiable predilection for sucking the blood out of living victims or from recently buried cadavers, which they supposedly disinterred and used for their nutritional and ritual needs.[7] Moreover, their neighbors feared a form of symbolic feeding through casting an evil eye on the victim, who would then feel as though her or his blood had been sucked.

Because of these buda mythologies, the Christians generally sought to maintain a cautious distance between themselves and the Beta Israel. Their fears and suspicions, based on the hyena association, were reinforced by tales derived from scriptural sources. For example, the local Jewish blacksmith was liable to be regarded as a descendant of the callous Jew who forged the nails involved in Christ's crucifixion. Related accusations, such as the crucifixion of Jesus on *Fasika* and the ritual murder of Christian children by Jews, also flourished.[8] As noted, they joined together these supernaturally based narratives and created a multileveled system of confirmation. The Beta Israel, given what was considered their unsavory heritage, were thought to possess ongoing malevolent inclinations, passed on from generation to generation. These dangerous powers were assumed to be in their blood, whether or not they were aware of them or ever activated them. Although my interlocutors usually attempted to downplay these accusations against themselves, they never argued against the existence of such powers, and these buda beliefs will reappear in several snapshots to come, demonstrating their abiding strength.

On the importance of meat in the distinctions between groups in general and in Ethiopia in particular, Frederick J. Simoons writes:

> The manner in which an animal dies often determines whether its flesh is acceptable. For some peoples the flesh of animals that die a natural death may constitute the bulk of the meat consumed, whereas other groups reject such flesh. . . . Other groups go still further, prohibiting the flesh of all animals not killed according to ritual observances. Most familiar, perhaps, are the provisions of that sort followed by Orthodox Jews, but ritual observances are also found among other groups. . . . It was a special problem to us when on mule trip in Ethiopia, for accompanying us were Christians, Moslems, and one Jew (Falasha), and none of these groups would eat the flesh of animals killed by the others.[9]

In the Hebrew Bible, there is an explicit prohibition against eating raw, bloody meat or consuming blood in any way: "Therefore I said unto the children of Israel, No soul of you shall eat blood, neither shall any stranger that sojourneth among you eat blood. . . . For it is the life of all flesh; the blood of it is for the life thereof: therefore I said unto the children of Israel, Ye shall eat the blood of no manner of flesh . . . whosoever eateth it shall be cut off" (Lev. 17:12–14, King James Version).

Beta Israel repeatedly expressed their revulsion at the Christian custom of leaving blood in the slaughtered animal and even more so over their penchant for eating slices of raw, still bloody meat, considered a great delicacy.[10] The raw meat, they went on to say, carried many parasites that caused different kinds of diseases from which the Beta Israel were free. They likened the eating of raw meat by the Christians to bestial eating and considered them to be "blood eaters" who blatantly transgressed one of the central edicts of the Hebrew Bible. In the words of one of my interlocutors, "Christians will eat raw meat, like dogs. We say to them: you are eating like dogs; that's not good. We laugh with them. They say to us: You don't know, it's very tasty. . . . We tell them that if they don't cook the meat, they will have worms in their bellies."

For the Christians, however, human and animal blood is perceived in the context of Jesus's purifying blood, and the symbolic consumption of that blood is one of the observances that grant the believer entry into heaven. One oft-repeated allegation made by the Beta Israel is that if the Christians drink the blood of Jesus to achieve eternal life, they might even drink the blood of Christianized Jews after the converts died. One interviewee explained: "The Christians have a law that they call *segaw wademu* [his flesh and blood]. It is written in their *Wangel* [Gospels] that whoever eats the blood will go to heaven and there will be forgiveness for all his sins. So a little child or a man who wants to be a priest, they feed him blood . . . so we think that they take the converts, they take their body and their limbs after they die."

The Christians' consumption of raw meat was for the Jews concrete proof that there was truth in this story. The Christians are described by the Beta Israel as blood eaters who transgress one of the central edicts of the Torah (Hebrew Bible), an edict linked according to their understanding with culture and humanity in general. For the Christians, the conception of the Beta Israel as buda is also linked, as described earlier, to eating.[11] The accusation that the Beta Israel were buda, with all it implies in terms of invoking supernatural forces, was an accusation of eating: in their night guise as hyenas, they are creatures that show no respect for the critical boundary between life and death. This specific association is, ipso facto, intrinsically related to the Ethiopian taxonomy of human/animal transformative potential in its multiple manifestations.

Jews and Christians thus accused each other of eating blood. The Beta Israel abhorred the consumption of uncooked, bloody meat by Christians, while Christians claimed that the Beta Israel possessed magical, harmful "eating" powers. In both groups the sheer humanity of the other group was cast in doubt. This symbolic reciprocity was forcibly expressed in both the content and the phonetics of the following account: "The Christians would say to us that we are *jib*, a hyena, which eats people. So we would answer that they are *dib*—that is, a bear. Why? Because what does a bear eat? It eats raw meat, right? Maybe a mouse or something like that, they [the bears] eat."

Thus, intergroup distinctions were powerfully manifested by the act of slaughtering. The very act of slaughtering was a primary indicator of difference and proof of the necessity of maintaining strict rules of social separation. In becoming consumable meat, acceptable to the adherents of a specific religion, animals were treated with obligatory differentiating practices, which clearly marked the borders between groups. Moreover, the consumption of meat was at the crux of certain ritual contexts among all the groups in the region.[12]

Beta Israel interviewees, familiar with their neighbors' slaughtering practices, enthusiastically endorsed their own and expressed disdain for those of the

Christians, perceived as lacking sanctity. Slaughter was described in vivid terms and accompanied by many demonstrations of emotion. Their own slaughter was undertaken meticulously and with utmost attention to the relevant biblical prescriptions relating to the covenant between God and the believers (Ex. 29). It involved, among other painstaking rules, a quick and precise procedure that was believed to cause the animal the minimum of pain.[13]

The general procedure was described to me as follows: "The animal was led to a pit dug in the ground, above which it was slaughtered. Its legs bound, and its neck held over the pit, its head was turned toward Jerusalem. . . . The eyes of the cow in the direction of Jerusalem. . . . It is important that the head of the sheep and of the cow and of the goat will be turned toward Jerusalem, as in the direction of prayer." The slaughterer, standing behind the animal without looking at its eyes, performed his task: he made the blessing while thrusting a sharp knife at the animal's neck, making sure the blood flowed into the pit.[14] Although the same basic blessing was required for all animals, some people would expand the blessing for the larger ones. This was explained according to the understanding that its body would provide more ample nourishment. The passage from life to death was as quick and painless as possible: "Our qes slaughtered very well. The knife was not touched by the blood. It remained as it was; it was so clean afterwards. . . . With the Jews the knife is so sharp that the cow doesn't even hear that they are slaughtering it."

In contrast, the Beta Israel described the Christian slaughter as the very opposite. It was "too slow" and therefore cruel; the Christians were depicted as people who ate meat from animals that were not slaughtered in accordance with careful and caring rules:[15] "The goyim don't care that it hurts the cow . . . the Christians will eat [meat] slaughtered by any one of them, even children and even slaves."

Although the Christians recited a blessing when slaughtering, the blessing was considered short and inappropriate in light of their "barbarian," "nonreligious" methods.[16] The following description demonstrates the interviewee's meticulous acquaintance with Christian slaughter practices:

> But [giving] Jewish meat to a Christian, Christian to a Jew, Christian to a Muslim is forbidden. Because it's souls, right? The Muslims do "*bissimallah*" [in the name of Allah], right? The Christians do "*Basema ab wawald wamanfas qeddus ahadu amlak*" [in the name of the father, the son, and the Holy spirit one God] and then slaughter. The Jews say "*Baruch yitbarak amlak yisrael*" [Blessed is the King (God) of Israel]. That is because the cow was in her life; she had life. Birds are the same—a hen was in its life, so

everyone does his own blessing. . . . In slaughtering there are differences; the Christians, even if they find a cow that is already dead, they would still eat her. If a cow fell down and died they would eat her—even if she had died before. And also their knife isn't so good. We have a special knife just for slaughtering.

Beta Israel interviewees generally had a keen awareness of how the Christians viewed Jewish slaughtering practices. Again and again I heard about the popular church teachings that likened Jewish slaughter to the crucifixion of Christ and the frequent portrayal of Jews as the progeny of Christ killers, obliged to carry inherited traits of the murderers of God.[17] In rural Ethiopia, slaughtering was carried out in a public place, enabling passersby to witness the event. The carcass was then hung on a tree to drain its blood. In the Christian imagination, this act evoked Jesus's crucifixion on a cross of wood. The Christians believed that the crucifixion was a Jewish Paschal sacrifice, similar to the Beta Israel Passover sacrifice.[18] One speaker claimed: "[The Christians] always said to us: 'On Passover[19] you take a lamb and hang it on a high tree and stab it, just like you Jews did to Jesus.'"

Passover is of course an arena filled with tension between Jews and Christians in many cultural contexts. The conceptual circle revealed here is based on a mutual projection between a doctrine (the crucifixion of Jesus by the Jews) and a reaction to praxis (the Paschal offering). Each group expresses revulsion over the mode of slaughter and also the subsequent meat-eating customs of the other group.

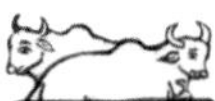

The Beta Israel integrated animal sacrifice in their rites; Christians did not. In keeping with biblical traditions, the Beta Israel made sacrifices as personal and community penance: a burnt sacrifice, a sin offering, and a Passover sacrifice.[20] In addition, they observed the practice of purification using the ashes of a red heifer, particularly in purification rites surrounding the dead.[21]

The sacrifice of an animal illustrates the nexus of exchange between man and deity. For the Beta Israel, the blood of the animal strengthens the covenant between God and Jewish believers.[22] The blood of the slaughtered animal is symbolic of the blood of Christ, whose bloodshed is understood to be the cause for the Jews' abandonment and the establishment of a new covenant between God and the followers of Christ.

This covenant is expressed by means of several obligatory regulations, starkly demonstrated in the Passover sacrifice. For the Beta Israel, this was the essential ritual of the holiday, capturing the drama of the biblical Exodus.[23] The reenactment included a wide array of activities, most dominant of which were the gathering of the community in the courtyard of the local prayer house, each community member holding a tall walking stick and a backpack as if ready to embark on their imminent departure. Days and even weeks before, a sheep (or on occasion a goat) was selected. The presence of the selected sheep generated a growing anticipation to the upcoming sacrifice and whetted the appetite for its imagined taste.[24] To ensure its suitability to serve as the Passover sacrifice, the chosen sheep was protected and pampered. It had to be beyond the phase of nursing and before puberty, blemish-free, and brightly colored. All these characteristics were meant to assure its divine acceptance. The earthly procedures included bringing the sheep in and laying it with its limbs tied over a pit dug or a stone altar set up in the courtyard. It was then ready for the qes's blessing and expedient slaughter. Salt was spread over the animal, signifying its sacrificial status. Branches were dipped in its blood and used to mark a sign over the entrance to the huts. Following this, the body was lifted and hung on a nearby tree, enabling the rest of its blood to flow out before being cut into small, edible pieces. These were grilled over an open fire and distributed among the participants for each to taste, accompanied by a qitta, the Passover unleavened bread. The inedible remnants of the sheep were then totally burned. For the Beta Israel, all this was a living reenactment of the hasty flight from Egypt. Christian neighbors, however, interpreted that same Passover sacrifice as being a living reenactment of the crucifixion. The use of the very same name—Fasika—for holidays commemorating the myths of origin for the two religions is a reinforcement of their inherent indivisibility. The tangibility of the Passover sacrifice with its visual characteristics and specific timing enables an intertwining of the two distinct myths over the body of one animal, powerfully demonstrating the centrality of meat in the relations between Jews and Christians.

Made aware by European missionaries that mainstream Judaism had long abandoned sacrificial practices, the Christians, as the Jews recall, were highly critical of the survival of this discredited rite among their neighbors.[25] At the same time, some Christians would occasionally ask their Jewish neighbors to perform such a sacrifice on their behalf. This request may have been justified by

the Christians on practical grounds, since they did not sacrifice animals. The
Beta Israel however, clearly understood this request as a covert acknowledgment of the special relationship between the Jews and God.[26]

Slaughter and meat eating were obviously pivotal in the arena of mutual
accusations, avoidances, insults, and suspicions. This arena, however, also
contained more accommodating attitudes and practices, indicative of mutual
respect and cooperation. The pragmatic skills displayed to reach out to one
another despite religious differences have never failed to amaze me, and in
such celebrations, meat was once again at the center. The balancing structure
of weddings, in which different and mutually exclusive groups were enabled
to participate without violating different percepts over meat, merits further
elaboration.

A wedding was an event for all neighbors to celebrate regardless of religion.
The uniqueness of the situation is succinctly captured in the following quote:
"If I have Christian friends, I can invite them [to a wedding]. If there's eating, I
give them a sheep or two for as many as are coming and they slaughter it alone,
on the side. Each one sits alone; also the Muslims eat alone. Then when there's
happiness and dancing, everyone joins together."

The wedding was divided into two distinct parts: the religious ritual and
the celebration. Generally, according to the recollections of Beta Israel members, the religious part was reserved for one's own group, and then followed
feasting and a convivial mingling for singing and dancing. When guests from
a neighboring religious group were invited to a celebration, the hosts supplied
the invited parties in advance with animals for slaughter. A special temporary
hut (*das*) was erected for each group so that they could dine separately (see
fig. 4.1).

This gesture enabled members of different religious groups to engage in
this crucial part of a wedding—the slaughtering and eating of meat—while
still respecting their own religious commandments. It was a multidirectional
means of displaying honor: to honor your neighbors by inviting them to celebrate together and at the same time respect existing religious distinctions.[27]
Nevertheless, eating at the wedding was not devoid of conflicting sentiments.
These recognitions were indelibly marked on each slaughtered animal. The
cattle slaughtered for the wedding crossed over from shared livestock to a reminder of boundaries. With the words of the blessing and the flash of a blade,
each animal became a focus of separation and avoidance.

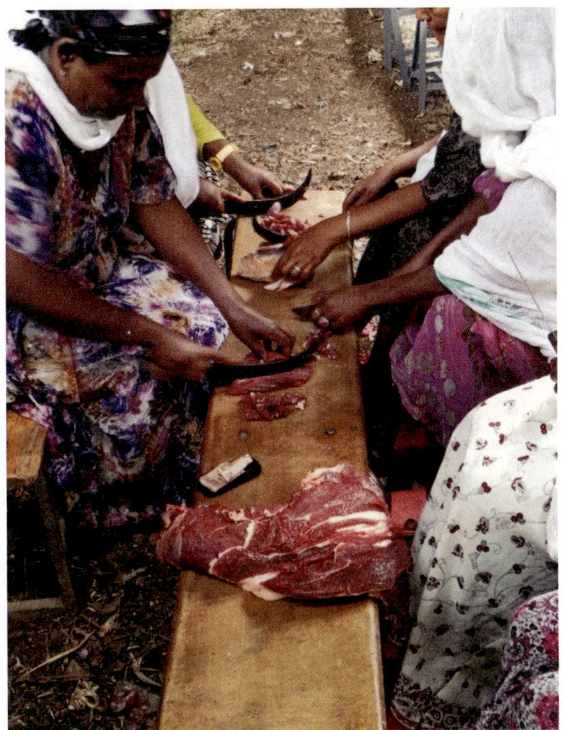

Figure 4.1. Neighbors co-operating in cutting meat in preparation for a wedding, Addis Zeman, 2017. Photo: Hagar Salamon.

Living so closely together, groups were aware of what other groups were and were not permitted to do and tried to cooperate as much as possible with their rules. Thus, for instance, when Beta Israel celebrations or memorials fell on a day on which meat was forbidden for the Christians, the Jews made available other types of permissible food. The Christians, I was told, took care that the Beta Israel could maintain their rules governing slaughter and eating: "They were very respectful from a religious point of view. They knew what is permitted and prohibited. They would not try to force us. They gave us everything we needed in advance." Indeed, both groups made efforts to facilitate their neighbors' inclusion in the ceremony.

Ironically enough, this penchant for inclusion among members of different religious groups fell by the wayside when the Beta Israel arrived in the land of their dreams, where they are part of the majority rather than the minority religion. As will be shown, eating meat at communal events and celebrations has become more problematic in Israel than it was in Ethiopia. The well-established accommodations that honored differing prayers and slaughtering practices ended abruptly in Israel. The sensitive attention to balancing traditions has lapsed, and the revered Ethiopian custom of groups eating alone while celebrating together has come under attack in unanticipated ways.

Years later, and with these accounts in mind, I had the opportunity to live in Ethiopia through the entire Christian Lenten period culminating with the feast of Easter (Fasika). This span of time included the growing intensity of anticipation prior to Fasika. The following personal account, an indispensable segment of the overall montage, is located both within and without the main themes of this book.

A central feature of Ethiopian Orthodox Christianity is the extensive number of fasting days that punctuate the year.[28] It has been pointed out that in regard to the number and severity of the prescribed yearly fasts and the scope of the restrictions that are placed on eating, the Ethiopian church has no rival. The customs followed by Christian Ethiopians are, in the words of Donald Levine, "probably the strictest in the world."[29] At the pinnacle of all the various fasts stands that of Lent. It lasts for a period of eight weeks prior to Fasika. And as if this is not enough, the Christians observe a separate three-day fast in the week before Lent. During the extended Lenten fast of fifty-six days, no meat, fowl, milk, or eggs may be eaten, and other foods are only taken from the early afternoon onward. Devout persons are even stricter and won't drink water before midday. This lengthy period is capped by two days of total abstinence from Good Friday until about three o'clock in the morning of Easter Sunday, after which they break the fast. The centrality of the Lenten fast is astutely captured in the recent work of the anthropologist Tom Boylston, who begins his account by stating that "the Lenten fast and its culmination in the Easter feast is the archetype and centerpiece of the fasting and feasting year."[30]

Beta Israel interviewees often recalled their Christian neighbors' holidays, mainly when speaking of their own holidays. Thus, I was fairly well informed about the Christians' observance of Fasika, especially its public aspects. Since Fasika is a commemoration and reenactment of the mythical series of events that separate the two religions, in Ethiopia as in other cultural contexts it played a central role in the conflictual relations between Judaism and Christianity and between Jewish and Christian neighbors.[31] It was Fasika—both Jewish and

Christian—that dominated recollections of holidays and intergroup relations. Despite all I had heard, I was still overwhelmed by the actual spectacle and absorbing ambience that I experienced firsthand in Northwest Ethiopia and Addis Ababa during the Fasika holidays. The eight long weeks on a debilitating diet seem to stimulate an ever-increasing craving for, in the words of Boylston, "a superabundance of meat and drink on Easter Sunday" to revitalize the body and social connections. According to him, this abstinence from meat over the long course of Lent stimulates a profound longing.[32] I tangibly sensed the growing intensity of the concern about meat as the fast progressed. The small butchery stalls had for weeks been either closed or open but strikingly empty, their wooden frames completely bare. As we approached Easter week, fantasies of meat dominated conversations I held with Ethiopian friends. Anticipatory smells and tastes of favorite meat dishes, accompanied by intricate details of the culinary preparation of chicken, sheep, and cattle and the pungent spices to be added to each dish, were constantly being discussed. Their imminent consumption made the participants ready to join together and share in a gustatory heavenly repast. Soon after Lent, the butcheries (*Siguya*) provided a myriad of captivating images. With the interweaving of dripping corpses and enthusiastic customers eagerly buying up the meat, the boundaries between belief and actual behaviors seemed to collapse, allowing me to conjecture the psychological and emotional implications of the Fasika-inspired purchase and consumption of such huge quantities of fresh meat. Next are two additional snapshots taken in Addis Ababa before and during Fasika.

The intertwining of the resurrection of Christ and the revival of the permission to consume meat was publicly articulated in manifold forms. On reaching Fasika, the totality of the mythical reenactment was palpable: the passion for Christ and the passion for meat became one. Surprisingly, this intertwining leaped out at me every time I passed one of the many butcheries exposing what I perceived as striking, iconic images of crucifixion. Addis Ababa was replete with an abundance of small butcheries, each typically displaying a single, fresh bloody slab hanging on a white wooden frame.[33]

The butcher stalls marked themselves as Christian with a large Ethiopian cross, usually painted in red on the front wall.[34] With the freshly slaughtered animal limbs outstretched as if on a crucifix, the effect was a mutually reinforcing set of images. Thus, each customer was enabled to share the flesh of that particular "crucified" animal. This would suggest, even if it is seldom acknowledged, that every morsel of meat was imbued with a sacrificial flavor. This impression gains credibility, I believe, from the following visual documentation of Christian butcheries taken during my stay in Addis Ababa (see fig. 4.2 and 4.3).

Figure 4.2. Displays of meat, Christian butcheries, Addis Ababa, 2015. Photo: Hagar Salamon.

Figure 4.3. A sheep on display on Fasika, Christian butchery, Addis Ababa, 2015. Photo: Hagar Salamon.

The snapshot presented and analyzed above is an integral part of a panorama filled with practices and vivid images expressing the unique rhythm and strict regime of meat consumption. A wide-angle exposure is called for, covering the days before, during, and immediately after Lent. After a long period in which meat is permitted and many celebrations, especially weddings, are carried out, the Lenten weeks begin to loom ahead, and people show signs of separation anxiety. In Addis Ababa, where we stayed in the days before the onset of the fast, butcher stalls as well as restaurants devoted to meat (and beer) were packed with extended families and large groups of friends joining together for a lavish meat bash just prior to the upcoming two months of meat abstinence. From the onset of the long Lenten period, as already mentioned, the butcheries became dormant, and with their white, empty presence, they seemed to me silent witnesses to the mythical founding Christian story. This all-encompassing cessation of activities related to meat consumption extends until the last week before Easter, when the demands of the fast reach their utmost severity. Then, simultaneously with the final spurt of strict fasting, the city seemed to magnetically draw in countless animals (see fig. 4.4 and 4.5). The streets were filled with chicken sellers, their colorful living wares strung along a rod carried over their shoulders; sheep tied together were constantly being led through the streets next to cattle, ushered by their owners to the market or being taken away by their purchasers to their new and final destination. They mingled with pedestrians and often wound up obstructing traffic. All this was overlooked amid the frenzy of excitement over the anticipated purchase, slaughter, and consumption of one or more choice animals for the upcoming feast.

Walking through this commotion, I found that the roads and streets of Addis Ababa had become a stage for the drama between restriction and indulgence—and a huge communal reminder of the exemplary crucifixion. At the same time, the sheer presence of all these animals clearly reignited the longed-for taste of meat.

Amos (my spouse) and I were living next to a sizable residential quarter made up of a number of apartment blocks, which shared a common courtyard. We passed by the courtyard on Saturday afternoon, the last day of Lent before the onset of the holiday, and saw dozens of children prancing merrily around and petting the many sheep tied up throughout the courtyard. The children were romping with the sheep they knew would be slaughtered early

Figure 4.4. Sheep taken home by a Bajaj Taxi before Fasika, 2015. Photo: Hagar Salamon.

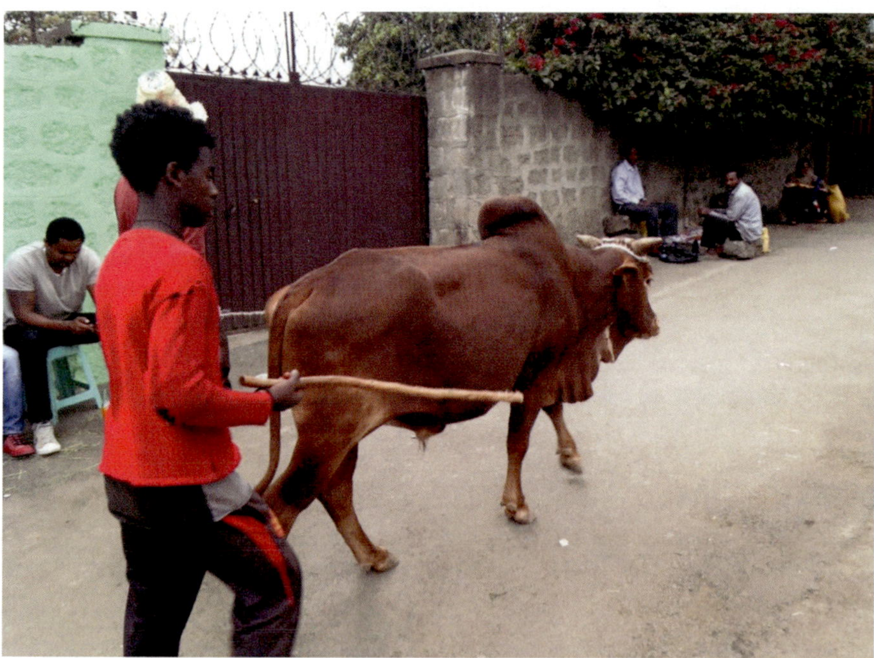

Figure 4.5. An ox taken home from the market, 2015. Photo: Hagar Salamon.

the next morning for the eagerly awaited Fasika feast. In the brief span between their arrival and their demise, the sheep dutifully submitted to being the living playthings of the exuberant children. Initially I was taken aback by this sight, aware of what very soon awaited the sheep and knowing that they would be eaten by the same children. As I recalled the long-term close relations between rural shepherding children and their families' livestock, this urban scene stimulated my imagination. On the way back to our apartment and still under the discomfiting impression of the scene, I remembered what I often had heard from my Ethiopian Israeli friends. When they spoke about eating animals that grew up with them, they explained that these animals were meant to become their food by God's providence. Permitting and even encouraging the children to play with the sheep normalized the upcoming feast over their flesh. Taking this scene a step further, it seemed that the children's play was moderating the shift from life to death and from fast to feast, as it simultaneously endowed each sheep with a joyful demeanor, making the joy of the children focal to the community's religious projection. This sequence of episodes reflects and contributes to the uplifting of believers and their chosen animals, who can be considered as jointly participating in a celebratory Easter meal.

Sunday morning, having spent the night before Fasika in one of Addis Ababa's huge and impressive Orthodox churches, we left the church well after midnight, when most of the worshippers went home to break the fast. The customary fast-breaking dish, which for weeks had been the center of so many imagined meals, was *doro watt* (chicken stew). This longed-for dish was, however, only the appetizer for the main Easter repast, for which countless sheep would be slaughtered at the break of dawn.

Fasika morning, the usually hectic and crowded streets were quiet. People were now celebrating with holiday meals at each other's homes, and the atmosphere was remarkably peaceful. As we walked around the city, aware of the solemn ambience, we began to notice ever-increasing activity involving sheep hides. More and more young children came out of their courtyards carrying the hide that most likely the day before had enveloped their lively playmate. The hide was now transformed into a mere piece of merchandise to be sold while still soft to a waiting merchant, usually a Muslim, who stacked his purchased hides in a fast-growing pile. The streets were soon filled with piles of bloody hides, and their ultimate removal by the end of the day marked the closure of this multiparticipatory, annual reenactment (see fig. 4.6).

Figure 4.6. Piles of sheep hides, Fasika morning, Addis Ababa, 2015. Photo: Hagar Salamon.

Once I had witnessed the powerful hegemonic position of Orthodox Christianity, the Beta Israel Passover sacrifice took on additional concreteness. I now realized that it was in the time of their Christian neighbors' severest Lenten restrictions that the Beta Israel, in the open, next to their own prayer houses and still in daylight, just before the start of the Passover holiday, slaughtered young male sheep, ate the meat, and burned all remnants. Suddenly this sacrificial ritual appeared in its fullest impact, and the neighbors' accusations I had heard many years before gained additional dimensions. The Christians constituted long-enduring dialogic and polemic adversaries. At the core of their conflict stood the unequivocal centrality of the suffering, crucified body. In this way the founding image was constantly projected on the nourishing, nourished, and deteriorating flesh, so powerfully exhibited in the Ethiopian sacred terrain. Religious practices stretching between sameness and otherness, theological conceptions and folk creativity, brought together in a confrontational manner particular manifestations echoing the act of crucifixion along with their attached doctrinal and cosmological images.

Notes

1.   While the group's actual origins are pertinent to the question of their Jewish lineage, their self-identity as Jews in Ethiopia was defined solely in relation to the dominant Christian society. Even in areas with many Muslim neighbors, Christian neighbors dominated the Jews' lives. In the memory of the Beta Israel, the Muslim presence was peripheral, with the spotlight clearly falling on the main conflict unfolding between the Jews and the Christians (Salamon 1999). For a rich ethnography of Amhara life in the highland plateau of Ethiopia, see Messing (1957).

2.   Officially, the Ethiopian communist revolution of 1974 brought an end to the leasing of private lands, but interviewees were adamant in their claims that they did not benefit from land redistribution. On the systems of land tenure in Ethiopia, see Hoben (1970; 1973); Crummey (1980; 2000); Donham and James (1986).

3.   For an extended discussion of these matters, see Salamon (1999, especially chap. 9, 83–95). My view of Jewish Christian relations generally corresponds with the understandings presented by Yuval (2006) and Biale (2007).

4.   See, for example, Honea (1956); Reminick (1974); Messing (1975, 396); Pankhurst (1990, 223–24).

5.   This belief, elaborated in Salamon (1999), was prominent in everyday relations between the Beta Israel and their neighbors in rural Ethiopia, with several terms of insult commonly used by Christians against the Beta Israel: *jib*, meaning "hyena," and *jiratam*, meaning "tail."

6.   On the hyena-man as a trans-African phenomenon, see, among others, Calame-Griaule (1961, 89–118); Dorson (1972, 3–67); and Herbert (1993).

7.   See also Dundes (1989, 7–32).

8.   Significantly, the same term, Fasika, is used in Ethiopia for Beta Israel's Passover and the Christian's Easter.

9.   Simoons (1994, 302); and as a boundary marker between Christians and Muslims in Ethiopia (Ficquet 2006).

10.   And see Barthes (1972) for the "pure state" and "bull-like strength" embodied in the French steak.

11.   For a general discussion on evil eye in Semitic folklore, see Dundes (1981).

12.   See Reed (2013). For an enlightening discussion of food in general and meat consumption in particular in early Jewish and Christian contexts, see also Feeley-Harnik (1981).

13.   See also Leslau (1951, xx) and Shalom (2016). It is interesting to note that the presumed pain of the slaughtered animal is recruited here in delineating religious boundaries.

14.   See Leviticus 17:11–14 for verses which deal with the relationship between blood and the spirit and with the prohibition from consuming blood. Verse 13 links this concept with the slaughter carried out by the children of Israel and with the covering of blood with dirt. According to the interviewees, in order to prevent

blood from squirting outside the pit, some would demarcate its boundaries with green branches. Directing the animal's gaze toward Jerusalem further reinforces the symbolic ties between slaughter and sacrifice.

15. See Leslau (1951, xx).

16. For a detailed examination of the centrality of knives, both concrete and symbolic, between religious groups in Ethiopia, see Leslau (1951); Salamon (1994a; 1999, especially 41–45); and Zellelew (2015a; 2015b).

17. Another example can be found in the Gojjam region of Ethiopia, where the term *damenenza* was a synonym for the Falasha, meaning "let His blood be on them" (Kaplan 1990, 154).

18. See Bakker (2013) on meat in Homer's Odyssey. For two relevant, sophisticated discussions, see Feeley-Harnik (1981, especially chap. 5), and Dundes (1989) on blood libel legends and anti-Semitism in other cultural contexts.

19. Obviously, the Christian neighbors used the term Fasika, which became Pesach in our Hebrew interview and is here translated to the English Passover.

20. On sacrifice among the Beta Israel in Ethiopia, see Lifchitz (1939, 116–23) and Leslau (1951, xxvi–xxvii).

21. Numbers 19. The last red heifer sacrificial ceremony documented in Ethiopia was carried out in 1952 by the Tigrean High Priest, Memhar (teacher) Abba Yitzhak. Its ashes were kept in a special clay vessel in the Tigray village of Bet Mahariya. I received a firsthand account of this ceremony from the late Qes Avraham Tezazo. See also Gunchel (2006). According to Wolf Leslau, who visited Beta Israel villages in 1947 and 1950, only male animals served as sacrifices (qerban), among them bulls, sheep, or male goats. The sacrificed animal had to be without physical flaw, and it was slaughtered atop an altar situated in the northernmost plot of the courtyard of the prayer house with a knife sharpened on both sides used exclusively for this purpose. After that, writes Leslau, the slaughterer, who was one of the qessotch (not the Grand qes, who did not actually perform the slaughtering) dipped leaves of several kinds of trees (two or four kinds) in the blood of the slaughtered animal and sprinkled it on the altar and on the entrance to the prayer house. Then, its skin was removed and burned, along with the blood and the internal parts including sinews, fat, kidneys, and bones. These were burnt entirely, and the ashes were thrown to a side place that was not stepped on. The meat of the sacrifice was washed, cooked, and divided among the qessotch and the people. The entire animal had to be eaten on the same day. Women do not take part in this sacrifice (Leslau 1951, xxvi–xxvii).

22. For an elaborate discussion on the "covenant of blood" in Judaism, especially in the rabbinic period of the first two or three centuries CE, see Hoffman (1996).

23. In distinction to the Passover Seder observed in other Jewish communities, this ritual-procedure was the core of the Beta Israel's reenactment of the

exodus from Egypt, as commanded in Exodus 12, verse 27: "It is the sacrifice of the LORD's Passover, for he passed over the houses of the people of Israel in Egypt, when he struck the Egyptians but spared our houses" (English Standard Version).

24. See also Shalom (2016, 145–50).

25. See, for example, Kaplan (1992, 162–63).

26. See Salamon (1999, 120). For similar practices and sentiments in other cultural contexts, see, for example, Patai (1986, 149–90) and Salamon and Goldberg (2016).

27. Guindeuil indicates that allowing Christian and Muslim Ethiopian neighbors to celebrate together while eating meat separately is mentioned as far back as the sixteenth century. The Christian mode of ritual slaughter, facing the animal eastward, is emphasized in historical records beginning from the middle of the nineteenth century (Guindeuil 2014, 63). For an interesting comparison, see Zellelew (2015a).

28. On fasting and the Ethiopian Orthodox Tewahedo Church, see Takla-Haymanot (1981); Larebo (1988); Isaac (2012); Chaillot (2002); and Appleyard (2010).

29. Levine (1965, 232).

30. Boylston (2012, 81).

31. For a broader perspective, see Yuval (2006).

32. Boylston's fascinating research carried out in Zege offers an extended description of Ethiopian Christian Orthodox fasting and feasting, along with a ritualistic-religious analysis. He observed: "I have tried to evoke the phenomenal and sensory potency of the long and arduous fast followed by the outburst of plenty: the experience reverberates for much of the rest of the year, and it is of course the length and difficulty of the fast that makes the ensuing feast so powerful" (Boylston 2012, 88). See also Boylston (2013) and Zellelew (2014) for a highly relevant study that bolsters these observations.

33. This omnipresence of freshly slaughtered, bloody animals in the central streets and squares of Addis Ababa is far removed from the industrial meat market. Awareness of essential differences in connecting the actual animal to the meat consumed is the lynch pin of much of the literature on meat and culture. For a detailed overview of "Ancient and Modern Approaches to Meat, Animals, and Civilization," see Reed (2013).

34. For a highly illuminating study of the Ethiopian cross and its symbolic meanings, see Korabiewicz (1973) and recently Evangelatou (2013).

Transpositions and Splitting

Under New Hegemonies

Taking leave of the urban public squares of Addis Ababa, we once again turn our lens to the Ethiopian Jewish community in its new home in Israel. The Ethiopian Israeli community is constantly celebrating and commemorating. In particular, people are expected to participate in life cycle events, the most prominent of which are weddings, funerals, and memorials. A distinguishing feature of these occasions is the obligation to give money to the hosts, reciprocated at that same event by the equally requisite serving of meat. Hence, an ongoing circle is created, composed of monetary contributions by the guests and the reciprocal serving of meat dishes by the hosts. Beyond each specific event, and even beyond the wide circle of communal financial support that this practice generates, the mandatory consumption of meat unifies the participants in joy and sorrow. Thus, it can be said that both in Ethiopia and now in Israel, the meat eaten at such occasions marks and symbolically highlights the participants' belonging to an intrinsically supportive community.[1]

But this unity is splintering, and it is precisely meat, once again, that marks the split. The mechanism that until very recently created an impressive binding reciprocity has become a source of constant struggle and rupture. In this simmering cauldron, meat actually generates intracommunity separation, so Jews who never hesitated to eat meat together in Ethiopia are often reluctant to do so in Israel.[2] As a result, at the most important life cycle events guests are confronted with a perplexing maelstrom, at the critical center of which is meat. At every such occasion, the invitees now must examine the specifics of the slaughtering procedure and decide whether they will partake of the meat served. This is a vexing matter for the entire community, most noticeably among the older generation.

The foremost arena where these meat ruptures constantly occur is the Israeli wedding hall. The standard kosher fare served at such halls is under the strict supervision of a religious food inspector certified by the Chief (state) Rabbinate. Many Israeli Ethiopians refrain from all meat slaughtered under the rabbinate's supervision. These individuals will attend the wedding but sit quietly at their tables, abstaining from the meat placed on their plates. The most common practice is to hold weddings on a Thursday evening, eating and dancing until the hall is closed. The next morning it is customary to resume the festivities, continuing until sunset at a previously announced location, which may be the courtyard of an apartment complex, or a public hall attached to a local synagogue. Often the party picks up again Saturday evening after the Sabbath. These after-parties, like other traditional life cycle gatherings, are not under the supervision of the rabbinate. Still, many guests have serious issues to deal with, again regarding the meat served. Inquiries are made to ascertain who did the slaughtering. Although close relatives or friends who wish to attend such parties without facing the meat dilemma can request to be served *shero*, a chickpea or bean-paste stew, instead of a meat dish, meat tension is still rampant at every wedding party.

One outstanding rift in this context is between people coming from Tigre (called in Israel Tigrinim or Tigrim) and those coming from the region of Gondar (known as Amharim or Gondarim). In brief, the Tigreans abide by the Israeli rabbinate's procedure, while the Gondaris insist on following the traditional method of slaughtering that in Ethiopia was followed by all Jewish communities. To accommodate these differences, the host may serve the meat stews in different colored pots, indicative of different slaughterers.

Here I remind the reader that although the rabbinate acknowledged the Jewish identity of the immigrating group as a collective, it cast doubt on the Jewishness of each of its members as an individual. From the rabbinate's perspective, the doubt stems from the fact that the status of the community members was determined by the priests of the community, the qessim, and not according to the Jewish Halakha. This corpus of religious laws based on the Hebrew Bible and especially on postbiblical sources like the Talmud, rabbinic texts, and related customs and traditions was not extant among the Jews in Ethiopia.[3]

The different waves of immigrants from Ethiopia dealt with the issue of their religious status in various ways. The first groups, which came to Israel beginning in 1977 and continuing until after Operation Moses in 1984/5, were forced to go through a pro forma conversion. This process, called *giyur le'ḥumra*, refers to conversions performed as precautionary measures, undertaken when a doubt exists about one's Jewishness. This includes immersion in a ritual bath (mikvah) and, in the case of men, a symbolic covenant of circumcision (Brit Milah) in the form of "drawing a drop of the blood of the covenant" (*hatafat dam brit*). The "drop of blood" was drawn from already-circumcised males as part of their required conversion, the "completion" of their Brit Milah, even though they all had been circumcised in Ethiopia as commanded in the book of Genesis (chap. 17). A declaration of acceptance of the laws of the rabbinate was an integral part of this process.

The first wave of Ethiopian immigrants expressed no explicit opposition to this conversion procedure. Today, when converted members of the community look back, they explain the lack of opposition as stemming both from a willingness to compromise—to remove obstacles and become recognized on an individual basis as Jews in Israel—and from a strong desire not to interfere with the ongoing immigration of the members of the community still remaining in Ethiopia. Converted interlocutors stated that they submitted to the process due to a lack of precise understanding about the meaning and repercussions of the conversion.

Opposition to conversion began to grow, however, following Operation Moses in 1985. Based on the centuries-old history of their Judaism and the difficulties they had faced as Jews in Ethiopia, the immigrants, now a mass of thousands of people, positioned themselves against the rabbinate's demands for conversion. The climax of this opposition was a month-long demonstration in front of the offices of the Chief Rabbinate in Jerusalem in the fall of 1985, an unusual clash that attracted widespread attention and sympathy on the part of the Israeli public.[4] Although an understanding was reached and the protest ended, the personal status of the newcomers who did not go through the process of conversion was left unresolved, and uncertainties regarding Jewish identity remained. This created an open wound enveloped in pain and rage, leaving members of the group vulnerable in certain areas. Those who have not undergone the mandatory conversion remain in a highly problematic status with regard to marital law—which in Israel is subject to the religious authorities of each faith—and other religious issues. The struggle, both concrete and symbolic, between these members of the community and the Chief Rabbinate has continued, and the raging emotions have found expression in the realm of kosher meat.

As if these public struggles were not enough, the community itself has split into two main groups: a smaller one of the converted, comprised of those who submitted to the demands of the rabbinate, and a larger one of nonconverted, comprised of those who vehemently opposed the rabbinate's demands.[5] One unanticipated outcome of this struggle against the rabbinate is that Beta Israel members, who in Ethiopia were all united in their Jewish practices, can no longer eat meat together.

The political overtones of this painful split, along with its meat-related manifestations, have been further aggravated by the rabbinate's explicit policy since 1991 toward subsequent waves of immigration from Ethiopia. The major component of this latest immigration is the group known as the Felasmura, made up of descendants of those Beta Israel who converted to Christianity in past generations.[6] Following the mass immigration of the Beta Israel, they too wished to leave for Israel.[7] As part of the convoluted decision to accept them, the rabbinate took charge of their required, complete conversion (*giyur*). This entailed a long process initiated in Ethiopia and finalized after years of supervised studies in Israel.[8] In this manner, the rabbinate was able to realize with the Felasmura what it had failed to achieve with those rejecting conversion: to impose without any challenge the "proper" Orthodox religious path and to be in a position to execute its designated authority. This fully converted group has come to be the most numerous of all Israeli Ethiopian subgroups.[9] As a result, the rabbinate's authority within the overall Israeli Ethiopian community has been buttressed, adding weight to its dictates regarding personal issues, as well as slaughtering. At the same time, the positions taken by the Felasmura have further exacerbated the long-standing, painful intracommunity friction concerning whose meat is going to be served and eaten at each and every communal occasion. The following brief descriptions provide the general context for these tensions.

Due to unique formal institutional relations between state and church in Israel, in which the existence of rabbinic authority is based on the framing laws of the state (which in fact are based on secular principles),[10] the rabbinate exercises extensive power over basic aspects of the personal lives of individuals.[11] A central sphere in which this power is manifested is the certification of kashrut: whether food sold or served in public conforms to the rabbinic rules of permitted foodstuffs, which are especially critical in the consumption of meat. As has often occurred in Jewish history, kashrut rules easily turn into symbols and mechanisms defining and distinguishing communities and subcommunities.

Many Jewish Israelis, even without being Orthodox, follow some aspects of the kashrut rules, while overlooking or being lenient with others as a matter of personal choice. Ultra-Orthodox groups, on the other hand, impose on themselves more stringent kashrut rules. Only rarely have there been expressions of organized, open opposition to the rabbinate's control of kashrut, as took place among a segment of the Israeli Ethiopian community.

Here is how the rabbinate presents itself to the public: its website has recently emphasized the important place of kashrut supervision in its activities, and consequently the site dedicates extensive space to the Chief Rabbinate's meticulous supervision of the enforcement of religious dietary laws. It first outlines the statutory basis of its mandate (translated here from Hebrew): "The Chief Rabbinate of Israel is an authorized body in the Prime Minister's Office [. . . and it] operates under the authority of 'the law of the Chief Rabbinate of Israel' and 'the law against deceit regarding kashrut' as the highest religious authority in the State of Israel, whose influence is spread across the Jewish world in Israel and in the Diaspora."[12]

Then follows an explanation, in religious and even cosmological terms, of the importance of kashrut:

> "And ye shall be holy men unto Me" [Ex. 22:31] in order to pave our path to the achievement of our spiritual and ethical goal to be "a kingdom of priests and a holy nation" [Ex. 19:6] we must be strict and insure that everything that enters our mouth will be according to the commandment in our holy Torah. There is a close connection between the height of a Jew's ethical level and his food. . . . Therefore the Chief Rabbinate of Israel stands, every day of the year, upholding the boundaries of kashrut and works day and night to enforce them, under the guidance of the honored chief rabbis of Israel *shlit"a* [abbreviation for "may they live long and prosperous lives"] with the continual accompaniment of the members of the board of the rabbinate shlit"a and by means of the close surveillance of the members of the kashrut committee that are in its council.[13]

Before the arrival of the Felasmura, the unconverted members of the group constituted the majority among the Ethiopian immigrants, and their struggle with the rabbinate became a defining experience. A salient feature of this struggle was the refusal to recognize the authority of the rabbinate and eat meat that was slaughtered under its supervision.[14] Intriguing differences came to the surface. One telling example that I was given relates to the blessings before slaughtering. For the Beta Israel, it is crucial to say a blessing prior to slaughtering each and every animal. In contrast, the rabbinate *shochet* (slaughterer) blesses the knife and is then permitted to slaughter without further need to bless each individual animal. Such differences and their critical interpretation contributed to the reinforcement of the traditional mode of ritual slaughter, under the supervision of the qessim, as an act of direct opposition, while members of the converted group consumed rabbinate kosher meat, and their qessim were trained by rabbinate authorities to perform ritual slaughter according to its rules.

The basic differences between traditional Ethiopian slaughter and rabbinical slaughter are described in *Until Dawn: Ethiopian Jews in the State of Israel, Issues from a Religious Perspective*, a didactic book published on behalf of the rabbinate:

> The main issue here is a problem of kashrut, whether certain foodstuffs are kosher, whether meat is kosher. When slaughter is done independently there is a problem, and in our holy community there is an ancient custom that a "lamb from his father's house" or a "frida" is done, meaning that a few families slaughter together.[15] . . . It is obligatory for the knife to be completely sharp with no tooth or flaw whatsoever. . . . In Ethiopia this was less strictly observed. . . . Another example is the matter of meat that is forbidden to eat: there are various diseases and defects, which, if the beast suffers from them, disqualify it from being eaten. Forbidden meat is a big subject, which only great rabbis are experts in. In Ethiopia, they only knew about some of these laws. . . . Another problem is the purging of the sciatic nerve and the *Helev*. . . . in Ethiopia the meat was cut into small pieces, which were soaked in salt water, etc. According to Halakha, this method is not effective. . . .
> The result of these differences is that, according to the Halakhic sages, meat slaughtered and deemed kosher by the qessim is problematic.[16]

The authors thus elaborate a number of dimensions along which slaughtering animals in Ethiopia differed from normative (Halakhic) slaughter, each of which would render meat from the slaughtered animal unkosher according to the rabbinate.

As previously shown, the slaughter and consumption of meat in Ethiopia marked a clear and well-kept boundary between members of different religious groups. The Beta Israel took pride in their slaughter, which was undertaken meticulously according to the biblical prescriptions governing the covenant between God and the believers. A prominent feature of this pride was precisely the conscientious use of a razor-sharp knife, presented in contrast to the Christian slaughter, which was too slow and not in accordance with careful and painstaking rules.[17] This example epitomizes a wide gamut of ironical instances in which the very considerations that in Ethiopia marked the distinction between their "kosher" slaughter and that of the unkosher Christian slaughter have been applied in reverse by the rabbinate's dismissing traditional Ethiopian Jewish slaughtering. This, obviously, has inflamed and perpetuated the bitter controversy.

Thus, the division between traditional slaughter and slaughter according to rabbinical Halakha in Israel parallels lines of separation between different religious groups in Ethiopia. Just as in Ethiopia, meat slaughter and consumption constituted a marker of the true or correct religiosity of each group, in Israel meat has come to signify the struggle between the Jewishness of the Beta Israel in relation to that which the rabbinate has sought to impose on them. This parallel was emphatically expressed by some interviewees with the opinion that Orthodox rabbis were Christians, who made latter-day changes to the laws of the Orit. From another direction, Rabbi Haim Vaknin, a rabbi in charge of a municipal slaughterhouse, explains why qessim are not allowed to slaughter in Israel: "A person who does not know the quality of slaughter cannot slaughter, regardless of his origin. He can kill the beast, but this will not be a kosher slaughter. There is no discrimination here." Rabbi Vaknin claims that he can understand the stance of the qessim but cannot justify it. "It is no secret that it is easier to take the Jew out of the Diaspora than it is to take the Diaspora out of the Jew."[18]

This division over slaughtering has far-reaching implications for all sides. From time to time, reports appear in Israeli media on "Ethiopian animal slaughter." These reports often include terms such as "a grave phenomenon," "illegal slaughter," and "black slaughter." In a local newspaper, it was reported:

> Hundreds of Ethiopian residents have been endangering their health, after the rabbinate refused to let them slaughter in the slaughterhouse under the supervision of the veterinary service. . . . In particular we see the phenomenon known in professional jargon as "black slaughter"—slaughter of animals for the eating, which does not take place in the slaughterhouse or under the supervision of the veterinary services. . . . Some of the qessim have been slaughtering by themselves sheep that were purchased from moshavim

[a type of agricultural settlement] in the area, and all that under cover of darkness and in the groves nearby their neighborhoods. Usually the parts of the meat are transferred directly to buyers from within the community, but in some of the cases the meat parts are transferred directly to the butcher shops and sold as kosher meat. . . . Ethiopian residents of the city aren't interested in the various religious wars taking place: they want to eat their meat as their forefathers did. As far as they are concerned, they only trust their qessim to know what to do.[19]

It is worth noting the lack of awareness in all these articles of the wide-ranging expertise of Ethiopian born slaughterers regarding animals and their health. In an article from three years later by Shai Lotan, "The Qessim vs. the Rabbinate and the Municipality: Let Us Slaughter" (2009), similar expressions are used: "grave phenomenon," "illegal," "in slaughterhouses in the Territories [territories under Palestinian Authority] or in Arab cities in Israel," "not under the supervision of the Chief Rabbinate in Israel," "in people's backyards," and "what is known as 'black slaughter.'" And with a different emphasis: "People in Netanya claim that they warned the qessim about diseases and all sorts of trouble that can be caused as a result of this." The writer explains that:

> When they immigrated to Israel, they asked that the qessim [be able to] slaughter the beasts and fowl in the municipal slaughterhouses . . . but the Chief Rabbinate laid down a categorical veto. . . . "As far as I am concerned," says the municipal veterinarian of Netanya, Dr. Louis Horenstein, "I would rather they allow them to slaughter here. In my opinion, they are entitled, but apparently Halakhically speaking there is a problem with it. . . . We explain to the qessim that black slaughter is against the law, and they are insulted; they think we are racist. They don't understand that the term 'black slaughter' does not refer to their skin color. This is certainly a problem."[20]

Creating an association between the Ethiopian slaughter and "Muslim" animals (animals bought from Bedouins in the Negev or from the territories of the Palestinian Authority) is another problematic discourse found in the media. Such animals are not prohibited in Jewish law, but because they are not slaughtered under the supervision of the rabbinate, they are spoken of in terms of a health hazard, and the slaughter itself is construed as an act that borders on illegal and thus morally unkosher. Concern for the health of members of the community and the general public is a recurring trope in various publications, connected generally with non-Jewish slaughter in Israel, including Muslim ritual slaughter.

An example of this trope is the article "Journey in the Footsteps of the Meat," which appeared on an Ethiopian community website and describes how a member of the Ethiopian Israeli community crosses the border into the Palestinian Authority at night and returns with a sheep, which he sells to "innocent" Israeli citizens: "'There are rumors that many members of the community [i.e., the Ethiopian Israeli community] don't feel well and are sick and feel somewhat weak,' says one of the people in the Department of Agriculture, and it could be that this is a result of the meat they have been eating" ("Masa be-'ikvot ha-basar," 2009). As shown above, health concerns figure prominently in the Beta Israel's criticism of the raw meat eaten by Christians in Ethiopia. Thus, a familiar yet ever-expanding field of associations is recruited for the conflict over religious authority, which is played out using the body of the animal whose meat is destined to be eaten.

The struggle over meat continues to diversify, and in addition to traditional community-based slaughter, several butcher shops have opened in the past few years that practice Ethiopian slaughter. This evolution brings the resistance aspect of Ethiopian slaughter to the surface, literally out of the community's backyards, and forges an alliance between traditional slaughter and modern technological marketing means, accessible through well-lit public channels.

The newspaper article "The Way to Religious Independence Goes through Separate Slaughter," reporting about the opening of such a butchery, reveals the internal community expression of the shops' potential (Sanbatu 2005). The author of the article, Iyanho Farade Sanbatu, sees this as another stage in the establishment of an independent religious alternative that does not rely on the institutions of the state, part of the process of gaining religious autonomy from the rabbinate.[21] A further, heavy price of this split will hereafter be elucidated.

Yaakov Gunchel, a lawyer and member of the community, aptly describes the intergenerational crisis among Ethiopian immigrants in Israel:

> The delegitimization of the tradition and religious customs of the parents brings the war over religious legitimacy into their homes. Many of these young people refrain from eating at their homes because of the strictures of Halakha, which for them are unbendable.... The Torah's explicit

prohibition is on cooking [goat] meat and milk together in the same pot, so certainly having two sinks is not the essence of the law. The parents are severely hurt and even see these strictures as forbidden according to the Torah, since the Torah prohibited the addition or detraction of anything from it: "Do not add to what I command you and do not subtract from it" [Deuteronomy 4:2]. The youngsters are also not willing to eat meat that has been slaughtered by the qessim without the authority of the rabbinate. Furthermore, the parents are convinced that their children are erring in the observance of the commandments; they see it as a revolt against the religious authority that guided them until not long ago and a rejection of the tradition of the forefathers. . . . Young people who feel trapped between two worlds and do not want to harm either one of them find roundabout ways of dealing with the situation. Some of them suddenly declare that they are vegetarians in order to avoid direct confrontation with the issue of traditional slaughter. . . . The scope of the familial and social damage widens and will ultimately lead to the complete collapse of the strongest institution among Ethiopian Jewry: the institution of the family.[22]

Within the Ethiopian Israeli community, specifically among the nonconverted, family meals have become a battlefield.[23] Many children of the Ethiopian Israeli community have been educated in state religious schools and have internalized the views of the rabbinate regarding the Ethiopian community's Jewish identity and practice. The rabbinate thus enters the intimacy of family meals through meat issues, bringing the conflict between parents and children to the fore, as children avoid eating meat in their parents' home.

Young Ethiopian Israelis raise the discourse of kosher meat repeatedly in the various forums in which they discuss the eating of meat and family relations. The aforementioned publication *Until Dawn* calls for "unity" between all Jewish communities under the observance of rabbinical religious law.[24] According to the rabbinate, this "will put an end once and for all to all arguments and disagreements."[25] In this manner, in the name of Jewish unity, the Chief Rabbinate does not sanction the proliferation of any religious variations that are not under its supervision, and it battles variations of practice that might challenge the religious authority with which the state has endowed it.[26]

In Ethiopia, strict religious observance was above all the responsibility of the older generation, and young people were less meticulous. In Israel the order of practice has dramatically altered. It is the young people, studying in national religious institutions, who teach their parents about meat consumption when they return home. The meat fault line continues to shift, and the consumption of meat finds itself at the center of a painful split between young people and their parents.

Another painful refraction is the Amhara-Tigrean schism mentioned earlier. A powerful expression of the wider implication of division over the separation of meat can be found in the connection between the meat consumed, the one who consumes it, and the collective body that each belongs to. Consider the following views expressed by Tigray born Israelis: "So, I say, why does the government even need to care for them? . . . I say that those who don't eat meat [that was slaughtered under the supervision of the rabbinate], they should not be given [anything from the government], and those who do eat meat of Israel should be given. Right?"[27] And in another interview:

> She, my aunt, for example, bought a cow, you see? So a rabbi slaughtered the cow, an Israeli rabbi [by "Israeli" she means "not Ethiopian"]. We go to the Israeli rabbi. So they [the "Amhara"] don't want from the Israeli rabbi. They want to slaughter on their own. The Amharim from their Amharim, they want him to do the slaughtering for them. So they went and slaughtered a cow, and my aunt's husband brought them two hundred shekels worth of their meat for the party. He bought two hundred shekels worth of their meat. Already slaughtered, and then when they come, you prepare it and give it to them. So he prepared separate pots of this meat and separate pots of the other meat.[28]

The next quote insightfully portrays the painful split over animal slaughter and its impact on the unity of the Ethiopian Israeli community:

> Meat is a story. It's a real story. Because we, the Tigrim, came before the Amhara and then we were taken to the mikvah [ritual bath]. And we didn't know it was in order to convert us. We just thought it was the mikvah. Then two weeks later they informed us that we were converted. We just thought that we would go swimming in a swimming pool, just to have fun. Then all of a sudden, they give us a certificate that we'd been converted and that now we are true Jews, certified kosher [she laughs sheepishly]. So that was it. We ignored it; we said, "Well, it's not so bad." . . . but then along came the Amhara, and they were stronger, and they [the authorities] said to them also, come like a herd of sheep to the mikvah. So they didn't want to. They didn't want to, and so there were some demonstrations, but still it stayed that way. So now, the whole community is fighting [against each other] . . . ,
> now they are making separations in the food. Some of the honor of the Amhara qessim was hurt; they said that their honor was damaged because

in Ethiopia they alone could slaughter the meat and perform marriages, so why should they be rejected here? So the Amhara here continue to slaughter their own meat and prepare it for themselves while we go to the butcher: either an Israeli butcher or an Ethiopian butcher with authorization from the rabbinate.[29]

The transformation of divisions over meat, from separating Jews and non-Jews in Ethiopia to intracommunal separation and even antagonism in Israel, is associated with the inflamed issue of the Israeli rabbinate's demand for conversion. As already pointed out, this demand divided the Ethiopian Jewish community to converted and nonconverted and opened the door for recurring recriminations. The split within the community between "Tigrim" and "Amharim"[30] reflects the chronological order of their immigration. The rabbinic demand that Ethiopians convert in order to clarify their personal status, to which the Tigrim, who were the first to arrive in large numbers to Israel, submitted, was later stalwartly opposed by the Amharim. This issue, with its inherent elements of honor and dignity, prevents people from being able to eat together and remains at the crux of an internal split within the Ethiopian Israeli community.

Taken together, all these testimonies signify the gravity of the meat split within the community, highlighted in the use of the introductory expression quoted above as "a story, a real story." The act of conversion placed flesh as a focus of meaning—both through the mikvah and through the mark of the covenant in the flesh—in distinct ways, concrete and symbolic. It marked on the flesh of the Tigrim their submission to the rabbinate with all the humiliation it entailed. Their modification into kosher Jews acceptable for the rabbinate, in the words of the speaker, goes through a symbolization not lacking in cannibalistic tones in the attitudes of the two groups toward the meat consumed and the charged act of its slaughter. While the Tigrim now refuse to eat meat not slaughtered by rabbinate-authorized butchers, the Amhara boycott the kosher Tigrim's meat.

The expressions "certified kosher" and "like a herd of sheep to the mikvah" add another layer of symbolization to the narrative of the intracommunity divide and its connection with the slaughter and consumption of meat. The point of no return that the unwitting submersion marked on the bodies of those immersed became an act of violation that seared the "certified kosher" stamp on the flesh of every one of them. Thus, the connection between slaughter and eating of meat, and between conversion and the two-fold split that it engendered, recurred time and again in this and other interviews. Memories of the act of conversion connect with familiar practices of separation between religious groups in Ethiopia. And indeed, as these testimonies indicate, the schism in religious authority exacts a high price on the unity of the Ethiopian Israeli community.[31]

When I read the following report of events that took place in a specific community center (in the city Rishon LeZion), I found the eruption of yet another schism of great relevance to the materials presented in the above snapshots. The report appeared in the Hebrew Amharic newspaper *Yediot Negat* (*Morning News*). It is presented with all its details in order to reveal the nuanced terminology that pervades this new manifestation of the above-mentioned meat splits.[32]

The social activity club Rishon LeZion serves the Ethiopian community as a place for celebrations and gatherings during periods of mourning. Over the years, there have been many confrontations at the club between the veterans and the more recently arrived immigrants.

The background to the division in the community is connected to the large increase in the number of newcomers who have recently joined. Unlike the veterans, the newcomers have been required to participate in a "Return to Judaism" program, supervised by the rabbinate. A key feature of this program is the obligation to eat foods approved of by the rabbinate. In particular they are taught that only meat that comes from animals slaughtered in strict accordance to the laws of the rabbinate is permissible to them. Meat from animals that are slaughtered by the qessim, the Ethiopian community's own religious leaders, according to their traditional procedures, is not considered acceptable to the members of this group, known to the wider public as Felasmura.

Consequently, a portion of the veteran members of the community did not welcome the idea of incorporating the newcomers along with the veterans in the activities of the Community Center. According to statements made by the mayor's advisor on Ethiopian affairs, the municipality was issuing an ultimatum: either the community will function as a single body in agreement, or the operation of the Center will remain in the hands of the Municipality itself. He asserted that the majority of the veterans support the integration of the newcomers into the operation of the Center, and that the reasoning of these veterans is that the newcomers were brought to Israel with the advice and consent of the qessim, so there is no valid reason to object to their full participation in the life of the community. It is their right to eat meat no matter the kind of slaughtering, according to their own preference.

Still there remain veterans who are opposed to incorporating the newcomers. These veterans even organized a strike opposite the Municipality building. They argued that there is no place for the Felasmura in the Community

Center, so long as they refuse to eat meat that is coming from the slaughtering done by the qessim. According to this group, the Felasmura's behavior is an insult to the authentic traditions of the Beta Israel.

In contrast, the supporters of integration from among the veterans argue that the Center was established for the use of the entire community. They remind the others that integration was agreed upon at the other Community Center in the city, located in the Ramat-Eliahu neighborhood. There an arrangement was agreed upon according to which the entire kitchen and the refrigerators in the Center were divided so that each of the parties had access to its own facilities.

The report ends with the hope for a solution that will allow the community to gain back its own responsibility for handling community affairs, and may even create an opportunity for cooperative efforts between the newcomers and veterans in other areas as well.

Notes

1. For a study of another monetary circle, see Salamon, Kaplan, and Goldberg (2009).

2. According to interviewees from various and scattered regions, it was customary practice, especially during weddings, memorial ceremonies, and major holidays, that Beta Israel people would share meat with each other without hesitation, fully accepting the slaughtering practices in the different areas.

3. See, for example, Waldman (1989); Corinaldi (1998); Kaplan and Salamon (2004).

4. Kaplan (1988).

5. See Salamon (2008a; 2015).

6. See, for example, Kaplan (1993); Salamon (1994a; 1999); Seeman (2003).

7. See Seeman (2009); Shabtay (2006).

8. See Talmi-Cohen (2014).

9. This group is referred to by a variety of names. See Kaplan (1993); Salamon (1994a); Shabtay (2006); and Seeman on "The 'Feres Mura' Dilemma" (2009).

10. The existence of an official rabbinate in Israel goes back to the time of Ottoman rule in the Levant. In the nineteenth century, chief rabbis were appointed in various cities as part of the millet system. The British mandate continued this system, while appointing separate chief rabbis for the Ashkenazi and Sephardi communities. The Israeli state continued this arrangement, designating realms in which religious law was to apply (for Jews, Muslims, and Christians), most prominently in issues of personal status like marriage and divorce.

11. See, for example, Friedman (1972; 1982).

12. Chief Rabbinate of Israel, accessed February 2013, http://www.rabanut.gov
.il/show_item.asp?levelId=61631 (site discontinued).

13. Chief Rabbinate of Israel, accessed February 2013, http://www.rabanut.gov
.il/show_item.asp?levelId=61631 (site discontinued).

14. For other forms of everyday resistance as suggested by Scott (1985; 1990)
among Ethiopian newcomers in Israel, see Schwarz (2001); Kaplan (1999).

15. *Frida* is an alternative term for a group of people that select an animal,
slaughter together, and share the meat.

16. Adunya-Adib and Rosen (2003, 42–53).

17. See also Leslau (1951, xx).

18. Lotan (2009). Notions of home and diaspora interwoven with complex
racial issues have been extensively studied in relation to the Ethiopian Israeli community with a special interest in related genres of expressive culture. See especially
Kaplan and Rosen (1996); Shabtay (2003); Cofman-Simhon (2013); Djerrahian
(2018); Ratner (2018); Webster-Kogen (2016; 2018); Greenfield, Sulika-Rotem, and
Weinstock (2019). For a discussion of the complex relationship between homeland,
home, and diaspora in Hebrew Ethiopian Israeli literature, see Mendelson-Maoz
(2013).

19. Nahon (2006).

20. Lotan (2009).

21. This practice, however, did not take hold, and as of 2016 there are no such
Ethiopian butcheries.

22. Gunchel (2008, 24–27).

23. For another source of family tension see Seeman (2015), describing educated
youngsters embarrassed by their parents' preservation of the traditional coffee
ceremony with all its spirit-related, magical associations.

24. Because *Until Dawn* was written for the national religious youngsters within
the Ethiopian community, much emphasis is placed on Halakhic issues, primarily
questions of Jewish dietary laws. In its practical advice on matters of dietary laws,
ritual slaughter and meat consumption receive particular attention. In the chapters
entitled "Keeping Kosher" and "Keeping Kosher in the Home of One Who is not
Knowledgeable in Jewish Law," which deal specifically with the topic of children
eating in their parents' home, the text states: "There are things that may not actually be kosher, for example—the meat can be problematic, as well as anything that
was cooked or heated in non-kosher utensils. In these cases, as painful as it may be,
it is preferable not to eat these things" (Adunya-Adib and Rosen 2003, 48).

25. Adunya-Adib and Rosen (2003, 45).

26. The particular issues the Beta Israel face in Israel vis-à-vis the rabbinate can
be seen in the wider context of what political scientist Shain (2019) has identified
as the "Israelization of Judaism." In many respects, the center of gravity of Jewish

life has been swinging toward Israel and its religious authorities since the establishment of the State of Israel.

27. An interview conducted by the author with a Tigrean woman.

28. An interview with a Tigrean young woman.

29. An interview conducted by the author with a Tigrean woman. On the centrality of honor-related views and terms both in Ethiopia and Israel, see Herman (2012).

30. For a detailed discussion of the manifestations of the split between the two groups, see Rosen (1987) and Salamon (2008a). Anteby-Yemini (2010, 53–54) mentions the intracommunity separation in the matter of animal slaughter, although she associates this division with the immigrants who came on Operation Solomon (1991) and not, as arises from the present study, as related to the opposition to conversion beginning as early as 1985. This appears in detail in Salamon 2014, and especially in 2015.

31. As already mentioned, a number of butcher shops using traditional Ethiopian slaughter methods have opened, not under the supervision of the rabbinate. This development raises the subversive act of Ethiopian slaughter by the nonconverted to the surface in an open way. Sanbatu's "The Road to Religious Independence Leads through Separate Slaughter" (2005) reported on the opening of designated butcher shops for the Ethiopian community where, in contrast to the regular rabbinical supervision, the qessim are those who certify the meat as kosher. The writer sees this as another stage in the disengagement of the qessim from the Orthodox rabbinate and the establishment of an independent religious arm, which does not rely on the state's institutions.

32. *Yediot Negat*, November 2011.

Candid Camera

Focusing the Lens on Lost Meats

The various components of the *Yediot Negat* that report on the divisions in the Ethiopian community center are creatively processed here in a series of meat tales, whose humorous characteristics seem to soften the harshness of the prolonged transitional status of both tellers and listeners in their new home, Israel. Reflecting on encounters with life in Israel by means of comical staging, the tales encode some of the more fundamental vulnerabilities of this group's dramatic passage and ongoing hurdles. The following three humorous tales take the reader directly to a highly popular and enjoyable cluster, which can be said to focus on the lost home and the lost self. The mislaid meat tales are enriched through the symbolic density of the meat idiom and its particularly humorous elaboration. The centrality of meat in these stories of apartment mix-ups illustrates the relationship between the immigrant's body and the lost home, highlighting scenarios in which meat winds up in the wrong place.

The first story, the longest and most detailed of the three, presents a comic tableau of the daily realities of life in an absorption center for newly arrived immigrants. The reader may recall the amazed description of the newcomers' competency in obtaining freshly slaughtered meat shortly after their arrival. In the following story, however, this competency is somewhat twisted.

In the Neighbor's Fridge

It was when we were in the absorption center. Someone had slaughtered a lamb. After he slaughtered it, he dragged it and put it in the home of his neighbor. He thought it was his house, but he skipped a floor. He brought what he had slaughtered, put it into his neighbor's fridge, hung his coat on the rack and went out for a walk. The one who put the meat in his neighbor's house goes back to his real house. The neighbor's wife returns and sees that the refrigerator is filled with meat:[1] "When did he have the time to go get meat?" she wonders to herself. "They probably gave it to him." At the same time, the other woman, the wife of the one who went to buy meat, asked, "He said he would bring meat—why didn't he bring it? Where did he put it? So what? Should I cook *kekk watt* [vegetarian sauce]?" The woman [who found the meat at her place] cooked it, when she served it to her husband, the husband said, "What? My wife bought meat?" So she said to him, "What? Did you not put it in the fridge? I thought you brought it!" So he said, "It's not me; it's not you. Probably the *ferenj* ["stranger," used to designate non-Ethiopian people] came and put it in the fridge."[2] The person who brought the meat wonders, "I brought meat; why didn't she prepare it? She's probably mad at me." At the same time, the wife of the one who brought meat wonders, "He told me he brought meat—how come he didn't bring it?" The neighbor [who found the meat in his apartment] identifies the coat of the neighbor [who bought the meat] and wonders and asks his wife, "What is this doing here? It belongs to the neighbor. Tell me, was he here all day?" And she says to him, "No, of course not. He was never here." So he asks, "So how is it that his coat is here right now?"[3] And so she puts two and two together: "It could be that the neighbor brought the meat, because yesterday I heard him saying he was going to get meat." The husband says to the wife, "It looks like you've done something, and I don't know about it." And the two go to the neighbor: "Your coat is in my house; what is it doing here?" The neighbor answers, "The coat is in my house—it can't be at yours." And then he says to him, "So if that's how it is, then I also put the meat in your house!" And that's how they solved the mystery. It all stemmed from the fact that they didn't understand that the apartments and floors were numbered!

Most of the mislaid meat stories, as will be illustrated below, are staged at an advanced point of the immigrants' lives in Israel. By now the characters live in their own apartments, purchasing and preparing food in their Israeli homes. Therefore, their continual state of bewilderment and uncertainty in regard to home and body stands in comic tension with their objective status as Israelis.

This Meat Stayed in Another House, and Others Ate It

One person brought [slaughtered] meat, got mixed up, and came to the home of others, which wasn't locked, put the meat down and went out. He wandered around outdoors, went back to his house, found some *shero* and kekk watt. He wondered to himself: How could I have brought home meat and she [my wife] prepared such a gravy? He went out again, walked around again, waited, and evening came. She served him the sauce. He said to her, "What is this about? I brought meat. First you give me kekk, and now again you are giving me kekk—where is the meat that I brought?" "What meat are you talking about?" "I brought meat and put it in the fridge." She says to him, "There is nothing here," and opens the fridge for him. So she says, "This meat stayed in another house, and others ate it. What is funnier than that?"

Set in an Israeli apartment block equipped with a refrigerator, the second story contains several allusions to traditional village life in Ethiopia. The external Israeli stage props appear as a thin veil over an essentially Ethiopian existence. The apartment door remains unlocked, as it would in the village setting, and the protagonist spends his time wandering around, as he might have done in Ethiopia; here however his aimlessness indicates his weakened status as an unemployed person. Then there is the menu, restricted to the two traditional sauces—meat or vegetable. The protagonists seem caught in a time warp between Ethiopia and an unfulfilled present.

Leaving with Half of the Meat

One person went to slaughter and bring meat to the house. He went, slaughtered it, brought it, came up on the elevator. He thought he had arrived at his own house, went inside, put the meat on the table, lay down on the bed, sighed with exhaustion and thought: Where did she go? She left the door open? While he was sighing, suddenly he turned around; the neighbor was leaving the kitchen where she was washing dishes. Suddenly he realizes he is in a different apartment. So she asks him how he is: "How are you?" He says, "Thank God," and all at once he understands the mistake and asks, "Where is your husband?" So she says, "No, he's not here." And so he says, "No, I just brought the meat so that we would split it." And so she says to him: "Thank you very much! You divide it; may God prolong your life!" And so he found himself splitting the meat into two and leaving with half the meat.

As in the previous story, this story revolves around the unresolved mixture between Israel and Ethiopia: apartment blocks, elevators, open doors, and slaughtered animals. This story describes the protagonist's conduct at home and his failure to recognize even his own bed. Moreover, he needs the mistress of the house to help him discover his mistake. The humor mounts as he tries to cover up the mistake and save face by resorting to dividing up the meat, leaving him with only half of the meat he had brought.

The sense of loss entailed in the experience of migration is miniaturized and metaphorized in these stories via key idioms. Prominent among them is the image of a slaughtered animal placed in someone else's apartment. The narrated images constitute a new chapter in the cultural and folkloric elaboration of the meat saga. In these stories I repeatedly encountered the image of a traditional Ethiopian newcomer, carrying his freshly slaughtered meat and trying to reach the right home. When these tales are framed in humorous form, they provide both tellers and listeners with a means of working through the pain and injury entailed in their experience of migration.

Having arrived in Israel after a decades-long struggle to be permitted to return home, the Beta Israel found themselves living in an ongoing indeterminate state. The abrupt, emotionally charged nature of the transition to Israel resulted in conflicts between the many dimensions of the self, as articulated in one's sense of the individual, of the home, and of national belonging. These conflicts lent a bittersweet taste to the entire process and to its personal and collective imprints, as intimated in the Beta Israel's humor.

Spontaneous intracommunity events, in which people share stories deemed and labeled as "funny," provide a compelling reflexive outlet. The participants, typically family members and neighbors, all share the respite that these gatherings provide. Often the stories told are already familiar to the participants, and the retelling of humorous anecdotes resulting in explosive laughter is indicative of their cathartic nature.[4] Vividly expressive of their encounter with Israel, the stories are endowed with a perspective on shared assimilation experiences, crystallizing in this unique folkloric corpus. Overall, these tales engender a sense of equality and a shared fate. They elaborate on the crucial question of the providential character of marital relationships. The mislaid meat temporarily jumbles the social ties of married couples, hinting at their potential instabilities. At the same time, these stories suggest hesitation about the stability and natural belonging of the narrators and their audiences to their new homeland. The above-mentioned strife regarding meat serves as a dynamic motivational background for the disruptive plots.

With lost home and mislaid meat themes at their center, the meat tales deal with the unfathomable shock of the group's relocation in Israel. The stories target specific characters as the butts of their humor: the elders, the newcomers, or, as in many humorous memoirs, the newly arrived self. A staple of many humorous scenarios is a depiction of ignorance attributed to the butt of the story, who represents the clash between a traditional past and a present involving a new landscape, time-scape, and body-scape. The essentially coded nature of the idioms in these stories does not detract from the reflexive work they accomplish, which is powerfully highlighted in the mislaid meat stories. I suggest that the transfer between meat and body, between slaughtered meat and the Ethiopian immigrant who is at the center of the stories, constitute profound, ongoing themes of vulnerability.

The specific image is of a slaughtered animal that is meant to be cooked and eaten but fails to arrive at its proper destination. As these stories show, variations on this theme use the image as appropriate metaphorical substitution for the perpetually nonarrived person. The slaughtered animal appears as a figural incarnation of the uprooted, bleeding, immigrating self.

In these stories the slaughtered meat, like the protagonist's body, gets lost. The metaphor is direct: the body of the immigrant is represented by the slaughtered meat, each of which plays out a drama of perplexed existence. This experience is stylized as a slapstick comedy of errors with a cast composed of traditional figures, their spouses, family members, and neighbors. All these characters are caught up in bizarre situations involving slaughter, cooking, eating, and even erotic allusions.[5] The tabooed sharing of private space with "the neighbor's wife" is punished by a reduction in the amount of meat available for oneself, consequently diminishing one's own body mass.[6]

A hidden characterization of prolonged distressful bleeding, of endless loss, of death without purpose, of the move from having to not having and from knowing to not knowing runs counter to the proper course leading from slaughter and ending in a meal. The crippling emotional load, both individual and communal, is represented by primordial images of meat, portraying contradictions between security and vulnerability, belonging and not belonging, intimacy and estrangement, order and chaos.[7]

Using the concept of slaughtered meat that fails to reach its destination, the mislaid meat stories profoundly illustrate the liminal state of Ethiopian immigrants in Israel.[8] It is no surprise, therefore, that the slaughtered meat gets "caught" in the story "betwixt and between": the one who slaughters does not eat the meat, the one who delivers it may lose it, and the person who cooks it may not enjoy it. The meat is consumed by someone who did not provide it. The modicum of acclimatization achieved by the central figure is signified by his competence in bringing slaughtered meat to his family. However, this competence is insufficient, for it cannot guarantee the delivery of the meat into the protagonist's mouth. The stories emblematize the liminal, perhaps even chronically impotent situation of the newcomers, especially that of the men, whose domestic role is to provide the family with meat. The incomplete transition from Ethiopia to Israel is subjected to a humorous cultural interpretation in which the immigrant inhabits a state between slaughtering and eating. Unable to consummate the transition, he remains helpless and perplexed. All three stories revolve around a blunder by the protagonist who is left with nothing to blame but his own ignorance.

The self-directed humor of Ethiopian Israelis serves as a vehicle for processing the drama of dislocation, touching on the vulnerable cores of its traumatic implications. In telling and retelling these stories, the participants mark themselves as people who have undergone a journey and a transformation, even if this migration is associated with vulnerability or a perpetually unmoored existence.

The stories uncover suppressed sentiments of loss not otherwise registered or expressed in direct discourse. The depiction of this core experience is manifold: temporal, spatial, and corporal. Images of the lost home and lost self are set within a backdrop in which the alternate realities of Ethiopia and Israel continually fuse and contrast. The tragicomic images that pervade the mislaid meat stories brought to my mind the painful account of Radai's party, which was repeated several times by different members of his family.

After living in Israel for more than ten years, Radai, born and raised as a slave (and now married to Habtesh, Mammit's aunt) arranged a party. Members of his ex-master's family talked him into throwing a bat mitzvah party in honor of his stepdaughter.[9] As already mentioned, according to Ethiopian custom, guests at a party give their hosts a gift of money, and when they in turn host an event, they will, in effect, retrieve it. To attend a party is therefore to give, and to host, is to receive back.

Radai viewed his ex-masters' suggestion as a compliment. The mere fact of their willingness to attend his party was unexpected and flattering. However, his party turned into what he took to be the most humiliating event of his life. It led to his becoming a near recluse rolling around in the dust in front of his apartment building, praying to God that his new-old oppressors be punished.

When his ex-masters persuaded Radai to give the party, they instructed him to prepare enormous quantities of meat. In a choked voice, he told me that they had tricked him into buying and slaughtering four cows,[10] even though in such events one animal is usually enough. The guests ate practically nonstop over the course of an entire week—among them his ex-masters and their extended family as well as the many neighbors who crowded in the courtyard of his apartment building. While the duration of such Ethiopian parties is typically defined and limited, in this case there were no boundaries. Radai and the women of the family did not stop cooking and feeding until all four cows, four times the usual amount of meat for a party of this size, were consumed entirely. And while guests typically visit only once, remaining at most from evening to the following afternoon, at Radai's party his ex-masters' family attended all seven days, endlessly gorging themselves. Moreover, the money collected from the guests was stolen.

Almaz, Habtesh's daughter and Radai's stepdaughter, added to the story:

> He ate it [got a raw deal].[11] They ate up every-everything. Whoever goes in there eats. You see it, [and] you can't believe it. Everyone comes, goes in, takes, and eats. Just like that, while they're preparing the meat outside with the sauce, everyone eats and eats.[12] Usually you need to ask permission, but over there everyone comes, takes more and more meat from the refrigerator, and brings it so that they'll prepare more and more for him. What's that about? ... Usually, whoever orders decides how much, but they [took]— more and more, just like that. For an entire week they ate and ate everything until it was all gone. .... He felt humiliated, scorned; he didn't eat and didn't drink, and stopped seeing people after the party. He felt awful. .... And, oh, how he would cry to God. He would go downstairs to our yard and even roll in the dust. To roll in the dust is [as if to say] that he wanted to die and be buried. There isn't a day that he wouldn't mention it. That's how it was for a long time. .... It ate him up from inside.

To my query about her spontaneous idiomatic uses of eating, Almaz answered:

> Exactly. Everything. As if it's permitted to take everything. Even things that it's prohibited to eat, they ate. I understood what you're thinking. They partied at that bash until Tuesday. And we can't say no. They keep going and going.[13] Thursday, Friday, Saturday, Saturday night, Sunday, Monday, Tuesday. How? Seven days! People were already driving him crazy. .... They said to him, "Do it. You don't have kids, and you're always going to other people's parties, so throw a party."

Radai's inferiority is signified through the cows' meat, devoured by an unstoppable flow of relentless, opportunistic diners. Space, time, and the entire ritual process are appropriated from him ruthlessly and with utter disregard. The aggression therein, branded into his skin, is innocent and naive in its total-ity. The wild celebration over the meat of the four cows loads this raid with significance, drawing attention to the symbolic and metaphoric meanings of consuming his flesh, permitted down to the last morsel.

Notes

1. Significantly, many apartments of Ethiopian Israelis are equipped with a spe-cial chest commercial freezer devoted to the quantities of meat acquired during the *frida* (and *kircha*). I imagine this is what was meant when speaking about the similar refrigerators. On Ethiopian Israeli newcomers' humor, see Salamon (2010, 2011).

2. The ferenj's virtual presence is a reminder of the state of passivity and de-pendency, as the protagonist suggests that "probably the ferenj came and put it [the meat] in the fridge."

3. The stories are spiced with hints of adulterous doings, including the refer-ence to the garment left behind. Compare, for example, the story of Joseph and Potiphar's wife in Genesis 39.

4. These humorous anecdotes are usually told as a part of an ongoing dialogue, in which the teller and listener take turns so that a teller becomes a listener and vice versa. The younger generation of Israeli Ethiopians also enjoy these events.

5. Deciding between meat and vegetarian meals is not an everyday choice. Meat is prepared for holidays and festive meals, while nonmeat dishes are daily fare.

6. An association between mislaid meat and eroticism occurs in various Ethio-pian folk tales. For example, Ethiopian immigrants in Israel tell a story of a hostess who hides the chicken she cooks from a guest visiting her and her husband. Later at night, she feeds the chicken to the man lying next to her in bed, only to discover that it is their guest and not her husband ("Chicken Dinner," in Alexander and Einat 1996, 75). For a comparison to the mislaid meat stories, see "A Tale of Two Fraudsters" (Alexander and Einat 1996, 84–5).

7. For example, the contrast between flesh and spirit is central to the interac-tions between Jewish and Christian identities in late antiquity (Boyarin 1995, 1–10).

8. In my use of the term "liminal," I am referring to the well-known concept, developed by Turner (1969; 1977), to describe the fragile state in rites of passage, where the person has already left his former status but has not yet acquired the new one.

9. It was not customary to celebrate either a bar or bat mitzvah in Ethiopia, and among Israelis of Ethiopian origin it is still not a custom that has taken root. It ap-pears that by their suggestion they were searching for an excuse to hold the party.

10. I heard the story a few times from different members of the family. The tellers used the Hebrew word for cows (*parot*) when referring to the animals slaughtered by Radai for his party. This is a common expression used by Ethiopian

Israelis when talking about cattle in Israel: usually no distinction is made between male and female cattle, and they are all referred to as "cows." I tend to ascribe this usage to the fact that unlike in Ethiopia, in Israel they have no prolonged connection to the living cattle and have only a very brief contact with the soon to be slaughtered animal.

11. The original Hebrew, translated into "he got a raw deal," is "hu akhal ota" (lit. "he ate her [it]"), an appropriate and perhaps not coincidental turn of phrase given the context.

12. In eating meat, barya and choa, as coreligionists, will eat from the same type of slaughtering. But the meat of the barya's body is signified as other. The randomness in this difference of principle is addressed in a complex and aggressive manner at Radai's party. The loaded encounter that erupts so painfully for Radai and his family at the party lends itself to a fascinating analysis in Appadurai's (1998) discussion of the concept of vivisection and ethnic violence. Through a comparative lens, Appadurai suggests viewing the expressions of violence practiced on the body of the other as vivisection, "a macabre form of certainty," a type of investigation of difference in situations of uncertainty.

13. A highly illuminating and shocking testimony of the Scottish traveler James Bruce, who on January 18, 1770, reached the ruins of Axum, northern Ethiopia, tells about "three travelers [Ethiopians] driving a cow before them. . . . One of them sat across her neck, holding down her head by the horns, the other twirled the halter about her forefeet, while the third, who had a knife in his hand, to my very great surprise, in place of taking her by the throat, got astride upon her belly before her hindlegs, and gave her a very deep wound in the upper part of her buttock. . . . One of them still continued holding the head, while the other two were busied in curing the wound. . . . They then forced the animal to rise, and drove it on before them, to furnish them with a fuller meal when they should meet their companions in the evening" (*Travels to Discover The Source of The Nile* 1790, 40–41).

Upraising the Vision

God Watches over Flesh

The story of Radai's party, with its heart-rending and sacrificial overtones, leads us back, by means of contrast, to the previously mentioned spectacle of the kircha, exemplar of equality and justice. At parties such as the one Radai envisioned, the meat of the animals, although cut into small pieces, is cooked in one huge pot and served by the honored host to all attendees. This form of division and distribution is characteristic of major life cycle events that take place only from time to time. For more routine occasions, a group of partners is set up to purchase and share a large animal. This divided and equal ownership with its customary abiding procedures is the earmark of the kircha. The following wide-angle ethnographic spectrum reflects both traditional rural Ethiopia and modern urban Israel.

Kircha involves the formation of a "meat group" to jointly purchase an animal for slaughtering, cut its entire body into small pieces, mount them in precisely equal piles (*medev*), and distribute them among the group's participants by means of a unique lottery system.[1] In Ethiopia, a meat group forms based on changing needs and circumstances to purchase an ox (from the herd of one of the participants or simply selected and bought together in the nearby livestock market), slaughter it, and distribute it among the partnering families. This elaborate form of sharing is reserved for large, highly valued animals and evinces a well-regulated, publicly displayed egalitarianism. Although in Ethiopia obviously performed separately by partnering families of each religious group, the kircha is carried out according to a similar template and evidently cherished by all.

The number of piles is a function of how many family units take part in the meat group. Each member of the group, with the agreement of the others, orders the number of piles he will pay for, and his request is registered on a list

Figure 7.1. Meat lottery, Tigray, 1977. Courtesy of Diane Lyons.

that is later used in the casting of lots. It was important for those who described the procedure to boast of the efforts made to include widows or single-parent households in the kircha. Significantly, their portion—paid for by another participant—is not taken from the donor's pile. Rather, it is gained, just like all others, by means of a lottery. The significance of the lottery was explained, then, in social terms, as a regulating mechanism designed to prevent the possibility of discrimination. Emphasis was placed on the familial and even communal benefits the lottery generated. As one participant explained: "This lottery is good so that they will not think about who will get much and who will get little. It is better than fighting, 'you took a lot,' and so on. So that there will not be an argument, everyone gets what he deserves from the draw." In this way, the equitable treatment of meat is used to express social feelings and social obligations, mutual aid, and community support for the weak.

However, it appears that this secular outlook ignores the transcendental, ritualistic dimension of the lottery, for it is not intended to create a winner at the expense of another. Rather, the defense and preservation of the equitable distribution of meat among all participants lends the entire ceremony a spiritual dimension.[2]

Traditionally, the head of the animal is separated from its body and green twigs are dipped in its blood (see fig. 7.1),[3] while the cow's hide is spread out on

Figure 7.2. The recently separated head, Tigray, 2012. Photo: Amos Salamon.

the ground in its entirety to serve as a surface for arranging its flesh into piles (see fig. 7.2, 7.3, and 7.4).[4] Once the entire slaughtering procedure is completed, the flesh, the bones, and the permissible internal organs are divided into small chunks and piled in equal heaps based on the number of participants. The body of the animal marks distinctions and patterns of sharing in the human society that consumes it.[5] The sole exception to this equal division is the slaughterer— a qes or another person familiar with the religious procedures—who is given the head, the tongue, or the hide. Thus, while all participants receive the meat in a form that blurs distinctions among the body parts, the religious mediator, in an inherently symbolic gesture, is rewarded by means of selected indivisible parts of the animal. At the completion of these two dramatic episodes, the participants are ready for the third step: the lottery.[6]

Termed *eta* in Amharic and *etcha* in Tigrinya, an elaborately conceived lottery is held over the meat piles to determine which pile each participant will

Figure 7.3. Distributing the meat into piles, Tigray, 2012. Photo: Hagar Salamon.

Figure 7.4. Meat piles placed on the hide, Bahir Dar vicinity, 2015. Photo: Hagar Salamon.

receive.[7] The meat lottery is a distinctive procedure carried out exclusively by men according to a set of well-known and precisely followed rules. Each participant creates a sign for himself by selecting a twig from a nearby tree. An identifying mark is made on the twig while the lottery conductor is either absent or present with his eyes closed.[8] One of the participants, or at times a young boy selected for the role, brings all the identification twigs to the lottery conductor. The latter's task is to drop one twig on top of each meat pile, without knowing which twig belongs to whom.[9] While the details may vary slightly from group to group, the format of the lottery strictly preserves common elements.

In a meat lottery I attended while in Tigray, the conductor dropped a twig on one of the piles with his eyes closed, and thus set the direction and arrangement of the distribution of the meat piles. At this stage, a notebook page bearing all the names of the participants was carefully torn and the name of each participant was placed on top of the meat pile due to him in accordance with the lottery (see fig. 7.5). In addition, in some areas, participants were accustomed to completing the lottery ceremony by eating a few pieces of meat set aside prior to the draw. At the end of the entire process, each participant took home his lottery-awarded pile of meat, to be carefully cleaned and cooked for his family.

Even among Ethiopian Israelis living in modern, urban environments, the entire spectacle of the kircha is adhered to, with people carrying out with great devotion and vitality complex practices far from mandatory in Israel's present-day meat market. Ethiopian Israelis consider meat as a cornerstone of their diet and serve meat dishes on many occasions. Nevertheless, they are loath to buy meat whose direct source they cannot see and touch. While they readily shop for all other products in the supermarket, it is considered unthinkable to buy meat there. The very sight of fresh, cut-up meat portions, or even more so, of frozen packages of meat parts, is considered repulsive. These sentiments, extremely acute among those who left Ethiopia as adults, go hand in hand with the ongoing allure of the kircha. In Israel, the kircha meat group, composed of trusted relatives and neighbors, is set up to purchase jointly an ox or cow in one of the nearby agricultural settlements. Following the selection and purchase of the animal, an Ethiopian slaughterer—either trained traditionally or rabbinate certified and, in any case, acceptable to the particular meat group—will be invited to oversee the kircha.

As mentioned in the introduction, I heard about this practice as early as the first months after the immigrants' arrival in Israel, but it was only years later that I became intensely engaged with the actual performance and its significance. I got to witness a kircha thanks to an Ethiopian born Israeli rabbi who

Figure 7.5. Performing the lottery, Tigray, 2012. Photo: Amos Salamon.

invited me to join a group of his friends for one. Awaiting us was the entire kircha spectacle, which began with long, deep eye contact with a living cow and ended with a pile of meat pieces, my equal portion in the lottery, wrapped in a plastic bag for me to take home. Due to my position as a researcher, being a woman was not an obstacle.[10] The wide-angle exposure that I witnessed throughout that day is vividly registered in my memory.

It was early in the morning and already exceptionally hot when I made the trip from Jerusalem to the southern city where my host lived. After gathering the participants from different locations in the city, we embarked in two cars to the chosen site. Outside of the city where they all live, in a windswept Bedouin settlement in Israel's southern Negev Desert, this tight-knit group of Beta Israel men was preparing for the job ahead. We parked our cars next to a shady booth and turned to look at the cow. A young black-and-white cow, which the participants proudly announced to be a shehar, was munching straw. Selected by representatives of the group a few days before, she was now calmly chewing hay for her breakfast.

Seeing the relaxed cow, I was suddenly struck by the prospect of the upcoming bloody scenes. Although I had waited for my friend's phone call for a long time, immediately accepted his invitation, and come all the way from Jerusalem, I was terrified. By the end of this all-consuming day, however, my initial apprehension subsided due to the highly respectful manner in which the entire kircha was carried out.

One by one the participants petted the chosen cow as they looked directly into her woeful eyes. In the meantime, the rabbi, now in the role of rabbinate-certified shochet, changed his clothes and prepared his tools. His razor-sharp knife would make the passage from life to death quick and merciful.

The owner of the compound, a Bedouin Israeli, provided both the cow and the site for the kircha. He had hosed down a slab of concrete scored to its edges with shallow, blood-stained channels and shaded by a tarpaulin against the blistering sun. Soon the time came for him to bring the cow onto the concrete. Mooing, the cow resisted, but with the help of the participants, the cow was slowly steered to a central post. After tying it to the post, they wrestled it to the ground, first on its knees and then on its back. The hind- and forelegs were tied separately. The cow settled down. The stage was set. All was quiet, almost as if both sides, the sacrificial cow and her ritual slaughterer, shared a mutual moment of silence before the impending act. The required blessing was pronounced, and the deed was expeditiously executed. As the body was still heavily quivering, the rabbi made every effort to reduce any prolonged suffering by quickly adding a few extra knife incisions.

I was struck by the genuine tribute her slayers paid to the animal before, during, and after she was slain. When the cow's final throes of death ceased, the butchery began. The partners began the dissection of the cow's body—a meticulous process starting with the removal of the skin and ending with the piling up of inner parts and bones. The process of dividing the body was long and thorough, conducted in a way that demonstrated equality. An especially moving moment was the sight of her still undigested breakfast, revealed to us once again after slicing open her stomach. It looked as fresh as the remaining hay that she had not had the chance to finish. The division into piles took several hours, and it was clear that all the participants were totally familiar with the order and details of the entire procedure. The cuts of meat that had been separated from the bone were divided into small portions and equally distributed among the mounting piles. The internal organs and bones were then similarly distributed.[11]

The participants went about this prolonged sequence with remarkable attentiveness, which seemed to me indicative of a deeply felt sense of performing a holy duty accompanied by joint gratitude to the offering cow. In fact, when I questioned them about their careful use of each and every piece of her body, they answered: "This is because of the honor of the cow." Being there, I understood "the honor of the cow" to have a double significance: the intrinsic honor of the cow and the honor they bestowed on her.

And so, the entire body of the animal was now reorganized into precisely equal piles and set on a wide table (rather than on the ground as customary in rural Ethiopia). The equality of the piles meant that every part of the animal was included in each participant's share. At the end of a long and hard day, numerous heaps of meat to be distributed among the partners to this cow's flesh covered the raised concrete table. The mood was elevated. The work was over, and now it was time for the lottery.[12]

The procedure was straightforward. Unlike the lottery I had witnessed in Ethiopia, where twigs were used for identification, here each participant marked his identity by writing his name on a tiny piece of note paper (see fig. 7.6 and 7.7). My name was added to the pool. The notes were then given to a blindfolded participant, who tightly and conspicuously closed his eyes, as he threw each note randomly on one of the piles. It was clear to me that for the Ethiopian born rabbi and his friends, the entire ritual was a significant source of pride no matter what modern Israel offers.

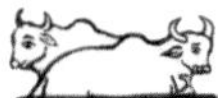

In the days and weeks following this experience, I was totally immersed in the challenge of deciphering what I had seen. Considering it from the broader perspective of the various meat-dividing and lottery procedures previously witnessed in Ethiopia, I found myself caught up in an elaborate web of reflections. Recent graphic images, odors, tastes, and voices, both human and nonhuman, met up with field materials from an array of long past, completed, and shelved research projects. What struck me was a result of the critical mass of materials accumulated over the years: a bricolage of sacred symbols, theological themes, philosophical speculations, and an occasional poetic flight of imagination.

The spark that the kircha ignited leaped out and set ablaze the many and diverse issues portrayed throughout this book. Over the course of that formational spectacle, my imagination was stimulated by the various stages I

Figure 7.6. Preparing the meat piles for lottery, Israel, 2012. Photo: Hagar Salamon.

Figure 7.7. After the lottery, Israel, 2012. Photo: Hagar Salamon.

witnessed. To begin with, the Bedouin host who provided the meat group with a place to perform the kircha was highly knowledgeable about their unique slaughtering procedures, reminding me of the close relations between the Jews and their neighbors in Ethiopia.

Watching the chosen cow peacefully munch on her last supper as each and every member of the meat group looked her in the eye while gently petting her brought me back to the many interviews where loving words were directed at left behind cows. The Ethiopian Tigrean shochet [slaughterer], who received his certification from the rabbinate, opened his case of slaughtering tools to bless his sharp knife. Watching him, I was flooded with associations relating to the enduring controversies and schisms in which slaughtering has been so prominent.

It was at the critical moment of the actual slaughter, and even more so in the following hours, during which the creature's body gradually lost its recognizable form to become identical piles of meat, that religious images flashed in my mind. Witnessing the long and painstaking transformation and sensing shared changes in the participants' mood, I felt that throughout the procedures, they were subservient to a higher authority. Jewish and Christian images came to mind. Foremost among them were sacrifices found in the Hebrew Bible, as well as the dominant Christian image of the ultimate sacrificed savior, whose flesh and blood are eternally being divided and distributed among devotees.

At the end of this long day, looking at meat piles with names of owners put into the car's trunk to be distributed at the different apartments of the meat group members, I could not help thinking with a chuckle whether or not the meat would reach its intended destinations. Finally, my thoughts were consumed by the lottery. It seemed that the efforts of the participants to do everything in their power to assure a just division were not enough, and a higher authority was summoned. Human autonomy was not sufficient to pave the way for the animal's flesh, whose transcendence of soul had not yet been completed to become a future meal, and the participants made supplications for the verdict of the divine.

In her book *Animal to Edible*, Noelie Vialles points out the great hardship of transforming an animal into food and the tendency for this act to take place in isolated, invisible spaces. Her study of abattoirs in Southwest France demonstrates the difficulties of transforming domestic animals into food and the complex system of avoidances connected with this transformation.[13] Animal slaughter in Ethiopia, on the other hand, takes place in open spaces and, in general, with a ritual gathering of a group of men. The visibility of the transformation from a living creature who shares proximate living space with the family into a tasty, festive dish raises many theological and philosophical questions about the system of connections and boundaries between life and death and between death and life—on the complex mutual relations between God and his believers, and between God, human beings, and animals.

Thus, the kircha not only demonstrates noteworthy social arrangements and sophistication, but it also projects a sublimated, even ethereal quality. Among the Beta Israel, the linked perception of meat eating and sacrifice is not limited to sacrificial rites. In fact, concepts of sacrifice, offering, and repentance existed in a variety of manifestations having to do with the slaughter and consumption of meat, embodying complex transformative relations between the eaten animal and the person.

Discussing religion and food, Gillian Feeley-Harnik offers a new perspective on the transformative connection between God and food as part of her ongoing exploration of biblical paradigms of binding, possession, and freeing. Binding and freeing appear in the formative scenes of the covenant between God and his believers, as in the central examples of the binding of Isaac and the binding of Christ to the cross.[14]

Applying this paradigm redirects our gaze to the complex system of connections between the cosmologically charged praxis in the lives of the Beta Israel—in Ethiopia and following their immigration to Israel—and the meat lottery, which stages the animal as victim chosen to nourish the partakers of its meat. However, this perception entails, if only by implication, a further interconnection based on the metaphorical logic of repentance or sympathetic magic according to which a transformation takes place between the individual and the meat.[15] The men's binding of the animal that is about to give up its life on the altar of their nourishment reaches heaven's door when the community serves it to God. The evolution from flesh to meat traverses the concepts of sacrifice, destiny, and moral responsibilities. Thus, every killing and eating connected to a holiday or ritual becomes a sort of sacrifice, wherein animals replace humans and are incorporated in them.

The meat lottery invites an analysis of the perceptions of meat slaughter and consumption from additional angles that may shed interpretive light on the web of prohibitions and allowances related to the Ethiopian handling of meat. The lottery, carried out after the slaughterer takes the tongue and the head for himself, directs our attention at the arbitrariness and intentionality revealed or hidden in this treatment. The perception of the slaughtered animal as victim, shared by Judaism and Christianity, enables conceptualizing a transformation between humans and animals.[16] With its collaborative spirit, the meat lottery allows for the collective processing of this transformation.

Moreover, the specific praxis connected with the meat lottery—with the chosen medium's abstention from seeing and the arbitrary allotment of a given pile of meat to a specific person through a plant pointer—is an interesting cultural allusion to the designation of burial places in Ethiopia by anonymous piles of rocks and a designating plant alongside.[17] This polyphonic echo between death and the raffled meat constitutes a tacit reference to the transformation between man and beast—between animal as food and human as food. The complex and charged connection of nourishment, in which flesh that eats flesh is fated itself to be consumed, is processed in the displacement practices of sacrifice and lottery.

The dense symbolism of meat among all the foods eaten by humans is signified in the substance of the food itself turning from animal to edible. Deeply imprinted cultural understandings and constructions relating to the building, maintenance, representation, and even challenging of identities, relationships, and basic hierarchies are assimilated into the private and collective body. In the many interviews conducted with Ethiopian immigrants in Israel over the years, in the different ceremonies observed, and in public forums that raise fundamental issues for the Ethiopian immigrants in Israel, the full power of the meat divide is exposed.

Notes

1. In certain areas where Beta Israel lived, this was called *frida*, which is used also for "slaughter to eat." See also Salamon (2017a).

2. In this context I would like to note the sense of pride that filled my interlocutors, and it is clear why: they felt the beauty and intense demonstration of social justice that lies in the egalitarian distribution of the meat. For example, when I raised the issue in an interview with a social worker from Ethiopia, it occurred to him that it would be possible to use this unique practice in Israel to reestablish feelings associated with intracommunal charity and equality. In the interview, he mentioned that in the region of Gondar, where he was born and grew up, a supreme effort was made to allow the distribution of meat to single mothers, widows, and the disabled. He said that special importance was linked to the eating of meat, and thus they took care to divide piles into quarter piles, allowing the weaker members of society to receive some of the meat. These gender considerations and empathy regarding meat resonate with gender-determined plowing practices guided by men alone, whose impact on women's vulnerability and gender inequality is well described by McCann (1995, 74–79).

3. According to a number of interviewees, these twigs are dipped in the slaughtered animal's blood and then used to sprinkle drops of blood around the entrance

to people's homes. This ceremonial procedure is intended to protect the residents and is familiar in a variety of cultural contexts. According to the interviewees, this practice was not unique to the Beta Israel, and their neighbors shared the practice. For the Beta Israel, however, it was associated with the biblical story of the children of Israel enslaved in Egypt.

4. When the number of piles exceeded the surface of the animal skin, green twigs are densely laid on the ground, and the piles are carefully placed on them without touching the earth. In a recent variation, noted in an open area at the edge of a Christian village in Tigray, the piles were placed on plastic sheets (see fig. 7.2, 7.3, and 7.4) photographed in 2012 in the village Berki, in Mekelle region in Tigray. I thank Professor Diana Lyons for her permission to use her photo from the lottery in 1997 in a Tigrean village, north of Mekelle.

5. For references to meat distribution into equal heaps, see Kifleyesus (2003, 563) and Pankhurst (1988, 178). For the complex relationship between human groups and their cattle herds among the Nuer, see Hutchinson (1992; 1996), and among the Suri in Southwest Ethiopia, see Abbink (2003). For the complex and painful link between slaves and cattle, see Salamon (2008a).

6. The literature does not address meat lottery among the Beta Israel, and evidence of its existence among other Ethiopian groups is very scant. One of the few sources is Weber's MA thesis, where this practice is described based on accounts he heard during field research among Tigrean Christians in the village Gulu-Makede (Weber 2005, 32–54). See Kifleyesus (2003, 563), Pankhurst (1988, 178), as well as Seleshe, Jo, and Lee (2014). According to Kifleyesus (2003, 564), unlike beef, with chicken dishes the different parts remain distinct. Social hierarchies are expressed explicitly in the parts of the chicken eaten by men, women, or children.

7. Respondents used the term "thrown" (*lehapil*) in Hebrew, bearing a direct connection to the practice of lottery. On the lottery of money and hospitality among Ethiopians in Israel, see Salamon, Kaplan, and Goldberg (2009).

8. The identification is created simply by means of a tiny mark, (such as to pull out the upper, the second or any other leaf) that each participant makes on his twig.

9. From an interview with a woman from Tigray: "Everything is divided into tiny pieces. The lottery is with names, you understand? . . . One man does not look; he hides, without hearing or looking. They call him and he throws [a twig] on each stack. There are leaves that they cut from the tree, one with leaves and one without. Each one is like this blade of grass. . . . Everyone gets a sign. . . . Exact piles. Everyone stays. He holds leaves and throws on every pile of meat." The use of a natural material was maintained in both Israel and Ethiopia. For example, at a meat raffle I observed in Tigray in 2012, while the names of the participants were written on pieces of paper that, following the draw, were attached to the corresponding pile of meat, the lottery itself was performed with the twigs. This choice marks the

involvement of forces outside of human control. Lotteries with similar elements took place in Ethiopia in other contexts, as seen in Weber (2005). For another significant lottery moving from Ethiopia to Israel, see Salamon, Kaplan, and Goldberg (2009). In this ceremony, practiced among Ethiopian immigrants in Israel, a kind of bank is established, and each month one participant wins by means of a lottery the entire amount of money deposited by all group members. For an elaborate discussion of cooperative groupings among the Ethiopian Oromo, see Lewis (1974, 146–49). It is interesting to note his observation that ex-slaves are accepted to these institutions along with members of other ethnic groups. In these groupings, similarly to the kircha described here, there is a marked and ritualistic emphasis on an organizing principle of "theoretical equality" (147).

10. For an elaborate, reflexive account based on her experience as a "marginal male" during fieldwork among the Beta Israel in Ethiopia in 1973, see Shelemay (1986, 7; 1994, 42–43). With this, gender issues relating to meat consumption are being played out. Most of the activities associated with meat are dominated by men, with women, as evident throughout the book, participating in different practical and symbolic ways. In general, gender-related changes and tensions following the move of the community to Israel are the focus of numerous reports, articles, and dissertations. These publications mainly touch on issues related to domestic violence, divorce, single-parent families, menstrual purity, the redrawing of gender relations, and newly acquired agency, as can be seen, for example, in Doleve-Gandelman (1990); Leitman (1993); Anteby (1999); Anteby-Yemini (2016); Fenster (1998); Weil (2004); Shabtay and Kacen (2005); Cicurel and Sharaby (2007); Salamon, Kaplan, and Goldberg (2009).

11. As already mentioned, in Ethiopia the skin is highly valued, sold, and purchased (see fig. 4.5). In Israel the cow hide lacks the value it had in Ethiopia, although the organizer of a kircha with whom I spoke a few years ago used it to make drums for community celebrations in Israel.

12. My use of the term "lottery" rather than "draw" emphasizes the fact that the practice involves the random tossing of personal markers on piles of meat, performed by a selected "blinded" person, while all other participants are at that moment passive observers.

13. Vialles (1994). For a comprehensive survey of the anthropology of food, see Mintz and Du Bois (2002). On food and transformation, see Fajans (1988). On food and religious transformation, see Feeley-Harnik (1995). Another relevant work is Fiddes (1991), which focuses on the centrality of meat eating in Britain and the changes that have happened therein, treating meat as a natural symbol, in a direct and purposeful reference to Mary Douglas's work on the "natural symbolic" connection between the human body and the social body. See also her analyses in "deciphering meals" (Douglas 1972).

14. Feeley-Harnik (1995, 567).

15. The explicit biblical transformation between a human and a slaughtered animal is offered in the story of Jacob and his struggle against God's angel in Yabuk (Genesis 32). The story connects, in a way that does not happen elsewhere in the Bible, the human body (that of Jacob) and the prohibition of the eating of the sciatic nerve of the animal (Genesis 33), which is a central tenet in Jewish slaughter. The same chapter describes the offerings that Jacob sends to Esau, a list made up entirely of kinds of animals and the detailing of their numbers, which serves as a reference to the laws of sacrifice in Deuteronomy (7) and thus establishes a sublime connection between the body of Jacob, the sacrificial offerings, and the laws of slaughter.

16. For an enlightening attempt to deal with human-animal dialectics, Deane-Drummond, Clough, and Artinian-Kaiser (2013) offer the use of a novel terminology. Troubled by the use of "human" and "animal" as opposites, they suggest referring to animals as "non-human animals." This idea was initially raised by Deane-Drummond and Clough in an earlier publication (2009).

17. Nehemia 10:35 says "[We will] bring the first fruits of our land and of every fruit tree to the LORD's house year by year." Along with the Book of Ezra, the Book of Nehemia was essential in the religious life of Ethiopian Jewry. There is a very interesting connection between this passage of Nehemia, which links fate and the sacrifice and marks fates through trees, and the common praxis among Ethiopian Jewry. On the centrality of the Books of Ezra and Nehemia in the *Sigd* holiday of Ethiopian Jewry, see Abbink (1983); Ben Dor (1985; 1987a).

8

Concluding Words and Continuing Questions

The Jewish world has long been fascinated with the Black Jews of Ethiopia. Their exotic existence as a Jewish group in the middle of Africa was pivotal to the inextinguishable attention given to them over the centuries by a diverse assortment of travelers, scholars, and rabbinic authorities. All these observers were concerned with questions regarding the Ethiopian Jews' origins and religious practices, which were focal in regard to the authentication of their Jewish identity. The application of these criteria facilitated the inclusion of the Beta Israel into the formative Jewish narrative without the risk of challenging its definitions and parameters. While their Jewish origins were an ongoing source of imaginative speculation, the Beta Israel's religious practices were inspected according to normative, rabbinical conceptions.[1] The result of all this inspection is a dual loss, obliterating the Beta Israel's long-defended Judaism and robbing Judaism of the opportunity to reconceive itself not through the imposition of external considerations of common origin or religious practice, but through an internal frame of reference, expressing the views and practices of the Beta Israel themselves.[2] The ethnographic perspective this book conveys honors the particularities of Jewish existence and challenges simplistic assumptions regarding an overarching physical and spiritual unity of the Jewish people.

Jewish tradition in Ethiopia evolved differently from rabbinic Judaism. While all Jews trace their religious lives to the Five Books of Moses, each community exhibits developments beyond what appears in that text. The Jewish way of life that prevailed in Ethiopia was shaped by singularities involving a unique religious context and a variant trajectory from the Pentateuch and the Hebrew Bible.[3] One telling example is embodied, as we have seen, in the nonhereditary status of the *qessotch*, in comparison to the strict hereditary lineage of the *kohanim*. In the emergence of the Beta Israel qessotch, religious leadership is based on a long period of study rather than delegated to a hereditary priesthood. This nonconventional path is most evident in the context of sacrificial traditions.

The qessotch, as religious leaders, crystallize their interpretation of the sacred texts by underlining straightforward meanings. As an example relevant to the theme of this book, Jews in Ethiopia interpreted the biblical verse "do not seethe a kid in its mother's milk" (Exodus 23:19; Exodus 34:26; Deuteronomy 14:21) in what appears to be a strict sense, while rabbinic Judaism came to see the triple appearance of this verse as the basis of elaborate laws separating meat from milk altogether.[4] The move to Israel, as demonstrated throughout the book, brought the Ethiopian Jews to follow rabbinic norms in this specific matter, modifying the role of the qessotch in the life of the community.

Situating this book in the context of Jewish cultures involves the inclusion of a different trajectory: the one codified by Beta Israel in order to bolster their belonging to Israel. The internal frame of reference of the Beta Israel, along with its changing dynamics, clearly reflects wider cultural contexts. This implies not only the broader cultural milieu but also nodes of interactions in relation to it. In the research depicted here, meat is both a powerful and flexible vehicle of such interchanges. While meat may be a natural symbol of such interdigitation, one would expect to find additional nodes of interaction in research within other settings of intimate religious contact.[5]

The book grew out of a gradual learning process extending over a period of three decades. The ever-accumulating issues regarding meat, and their repeated intrusion into so many topics dealing with past and present perspectives, marked them as a potent anchor of meaning and action in the midst of unprecedented upheavals.

Moving along the book's multifaceted itinerary, the reader has been led verbally and visually by a variety of snapshots: close-ups, wide-angle exposures, fadeaways, as well as selfies. Meat was revealed as having the unique capacity to accommodate and process—from transformations operated on and through it—complex personal and communal dynamics. Edible animals and meat appeared in a spectrum from the very concrete to the highly abstract. In Israel, the spectrum expanded to include nostalgic sentiments for the intimate presence of living animals and a growing internalization of their almost total absence in the new setting. References to meat, from the tangible to the poetic, appeared in ever-emerging venues, thus displaying their mediating capacity in regard to personal vulnerabilities, collective generousity, and mutual support, as well as communal conflicts and painful splits.

From their animals' capacity to work, provide essential products such as milk and dung, bring about social status and prosperity by giving birth, and ultimately become meat, skin, bones, and much more for their owners' benefit, Ethiopians derive a wide range of understandings, themes, and cultural forms, revealing the ample, abiding power inherent in meat matters. Despite the radical changes in every possible area of life that the community experienced on its immigration to Israel, and perhaps precisely due to them, the dramas attendant to meat matters have not disappeared, and meanings pertaining to meat likewise immigrated with the community. These matters are loaded each time with new energies evolving into cultural channels including sophisticated, transformative folk expressions.

As much as meat matters have been pivotal in my grasp of the Beta Israel experience in Ethiopia and Israel, I anticipate upcoming diversifications. In urban Israel, where the community encounters cattle mainly in digital form—in the many popular musical scenes filmed in rural Ethiopia and viewed on large plasma screens in their living rooms—the umbilical meat cord is most likely to unravel. In light of the long-entrenched centrality of meat in the life of the community, and in face of inevitable changes, one is invited to ponder the fundamental chasms between the two worlds.

Ethiopians give lifelong honor and respect to their animals while being generally tolerant of the animals' ultimate slaughter and consumption.[6] The traditional Ethiopian habitus in which humans and animals live so intimately together has led to a flexible and creative fabric by means of which people may contemplate in detail their entire experience, in its mundane as well as spiritual and religious dimensions, and creatively process it in various modes of expression such as rituals and narratives. Tapping into specific cultural manifestations as well as underlying human commonalities, the multifaceted undertakings portrayed in this book pave the way for a critical expansion of the meaning of Jewish life and for each reader—regardless of cultural background—to find personal significance in these meat matters.

Notes

1. The decisive rabbinic proclamation tracing the origin of the Beta Israel to the Tribe of Dan was crucial in the rabbinic acceptance of their inclusion as a Jewish group. In addition, various routes of migration from Israel to Ethiopia were speculated. See, for example, Kaplan (1992, 13–32); Corinaldi (1998); Waldman (1989); and recently Shalom (2016).

2. See Salamon (1999, 123–24).

3. For an in-depth exposition of a different biblical trajectory relating to the cooking of meat and milk and similar practices in North Africa, see Goldberg (2018, 37–44).

4. For a recent overview of this question, see Kraemer (2008).

5. See Schorsch's (2018) analysis of how biblical and Judaic laws concerning forbidden meat assume symbolic meaning in recent cultural and culinary trends.

6. For a similar emphasis on respect between human and nonhuman animals, taken from the attitude of hunters to their game, see Cahoone (2009), where he points out that hunters face the animals they are about to kill and take full responsibility for their death and butchery.

GLOSSARY

Abba—"Father," title of respect, also used religiously
Adera—A key concept, indicating moral obligations
Aliyah [Heb.]—Lit. "going up," immigration of Jews to the State of Israel
Amga—Herd of livestock
Amhara—Amharic-speaking people dominant politically since the thirteenth century
Amharic—A Semitic language derived from Ge'ez spoken in the Amhara regions of Ethiopia, previously the official language of greater Ethiopia
Amharim—Hebraized: Israeli Ethiopians from Amharic speaking areas
Amole-chew—Salt bar
Barya—"Slave," referring to both origin and status
Berberrie—Hot chili pepper
Beta Israel—"House of Israel," term preferred by Ethiopian Jews when referring to the group while in Ethiopia
Brit Milah—Jewish male circumcision
Buda—Magical concept of hyena-person or evil-eye person
Bunna—Coffee
Choa—Free-born, "civilized"
Das—Temporary hut
Dib—Bear (animal)
Doro watt—Chicken stew
Enbossa—Cattle from birth to three or four months of age
Ergo—Yogurt
Etcha (also *Eta*)—Lottery
Falasha—Appellation for Beta Israel, viewed by them as uncomplimentary

Fasika—Ethiopian Christian Easter as well as Jewish Passover

Felasmura—known also as *Feresmura* in Ethiopia and *Falashmura* in Israel. Descendants of Beta Israel who converted to Christianity

Ferenj—"Stranger," originally used to designate white Europeans

Ge'ez—Ancient Ethiopic, the language of both Jewish and Christian sacred writings and prayers

Gider—Female cattle after age three

Giyur—Conversion to Judaism

Giyur le'ḥumra—Conversions performed as precautionary measures, undertaken when a doubt exists about one's Jewishness

Gojo—Hut

Gondarim—Hebraized: Ethiopian Israelis coming from Gondar region

Goyim—Non-Jews

Halacha—Collective body of Jewish religious laws derived from the Hebrew Bible and subsequent rabbinic directives

Hatafat dam brit—Form of "drawing a drop of the blood of the covenant" to remove rabbinic doubt

Injera—Pancake-like staple food made of fermented, liquid dough

Jib—"Hyena," offensive appellation for Beta Israel

Jiraf—"Whip," made of cattle hide attached to a wooden handle

Kashrut—Jewish rules of permitted and forbidden foodstuff

Kebra-Nagast—*The Glory of the Kings*, Ethiopian national epic

Kekk watt—Vegeterian stew

Kircha—a group established for the purpose of purchasing, slaughtering, and dividing meat among friends and family members

Korma—Uncastrated mature male cattle

Lam—Cow

Law of Return—an Israeli law, which gives Jews the right to come and live in Israel and gain Israeli citizenship

Macha—Dowry

Maresha—Plow usually drawn by oxen or bulls

Mikvah—Jewish ritual bath

Operation Moses—A covert operation between the end of 1984 and the beginning of 1985 enabling some fifteen thousand Ethiopian Jews to reach Israel via Sudan

Operation Solomon—Israeli military operation in May 1991, by which 14,300 Ethiopian Jews were airlifted from Addis Ababa to Tel Aviv in thirty-six hours

Orit—Hebrew Bible written in Ge'ez

Qes—Title used for both Beta Israel and Christian priests (Plural: qessotch, Hebraized: qessim)

Qitta—A flat pan bread, also used as Passover (Fasika) unleavened bread

Qwanta—Strips of dried or smoked raw meat

Rabbinate—Israeli State Jewish religious authority

Samnawarq—"Wax and gold," a cherished indigenous poetic form characterized by intrinsic double meaning

Sanga—Castrated bull, ox

Segaw wademu—"His flesh and blood"

Shehar—Barren female cattle

Shero—Popular vegetarian dish primarily made of chickpeas

Shochet [Heb.]—Slaughterer

Siga—Meat

Sigd—Holiday of fasting and prayers unique to Beta Israel

Siguya—Butchery shop

Tazkar—Memorial service, a rite to raise the soul of the deceased

Teff—Indigenous grain-like seed cultivated in Ethiopia

Tejj—Honey wine

Tella—Barley beer

Tigrinim (also *Tigrim*)—Hebraized: Israeli Ethiopians from Tigrinya speaking areas

Tigrinya—A Semitic language derived from Ge'ez, spoken primarily in Tigray, Ethiopia

Tija—Cattle from about four months to between two or three years of age

Timqat—Epiphany, baptism

Torah—Hebrew Bible, in Ethiopia referred to as Orit

Wangel—New Testament, the Gospels (evangel)

Watt—Stew

Weifen—Male cattle after age three

Ye-Jiraf Ras—Lit. "the head of the whip," serves as a joint to increase whip's flexibility and strength

REFERENCES

Aarne, Antti, and Stith Thompson. 1973. *The Types of the Folktale: A Classification and Bibliography.* Helsinki: Suomalainen Tiedeakatemia.

Abbink, Jon. 1983. "Seged Celebration in Ethiopia and Israel: Continuity and Change of a Falasha Religious Holiday." *Anthropos* 78 (5–6): 789–810.

———. 1987. "A Socio-Structural Analysis of the Beta Esra'el as an 'Infamous Group' in Traditional Ethiopia." *Sociologus* 37 (2): 140–54.

———. 1990. "The Enigma of Beta Esra'el Ethnogenesis: An Anthro-Historical Study (L'énigme de L'ethnogenèse des Beta Esra'el: Une Étude Ethno-Historique)." *Cahiers D'études Africaines* 30 (4): 397–449.

———. 2003. "Love and Death of Cattle: The Paradox in Suri Attitudes toward Livestock." *Ethnos* 68 (3): 341–64.

Abdussamad, H. Ahmad. 1999. "Trading in Slaves in Bela-Shangul and Gumuz, Ethiopia: Border Enclaves in History, 1897–1938." *Journal of African History* 40 (3): 433–46.

Adams, Carol J. 1990. *The Sexual Politics of Meat: A Feminist-Vegetarian Critical Theory.* London: Bloomsbury.

———. 1992. "From the Sexual Politics of Meat: A Feminist-Vegetarian Critical Theory." In *Cooking, Eating, Thinking: Transformative Philosophies of Food,* edited by Deane W. Curtin and Lisa M. Heldke, 266–69. Bloomington: Indiana University Press.

———. 2004. *The Pornography of Meat.* New York: Continuum.

Adunya-Adib, Yedidya, and Yakhat Rosen. 2003. *Ad Alot Ha-Shahar: Yehudim Etiopim Bi-Medinat Yisrael, Sugiyot Be-Mabat Torani* [Until dawn: Ethiopian Jews in the state of Israel, issues from a religious perspective]. Or Etzion: ha'Makhon ha'Torani Yishivat Or Etzion.

Aeščoly, Aaron Ze'ev. 1943. *The Book of the Falasha.* [In Hebrew.] Tel-Aviv: Masada.

Alexander, Tamar, and Amela Einat, eds. 1996. *Tarat Tarat: Jewish Folktales from Ethiopia*. [In Hebrew.] Tel-Aviv: Miskal.

Allain, Jean. 2006. "Slavery and the League of Nations: Ethiopia as a Civilised Nation." *Journal of the History of International Law* 8 (2): 213–44.

Anteby, Lisa. 1999. "There's Blood in the House: Negotiating Female Rituals of Purity among Ethiopian Jews in Israel." In *Women and Water: Menstruation in Jewish Life and Law*, edited by Rachel Wasserfall, 166–86. Hanover, NH: Brandeis University Press.

Anteby-Yemini, Lisa. 2010. "Beshulei Ha-Nir'ut: Olim Me-Etiopia Be-Yisrael." [In Hebrew.] In *Visibility in Immigration: Body, Gaze, Representation*, edited by Edna Lomsky-Feder and Tamar Rapoport, 43–68. Jerusalem: Van Leer Jerusalem Institute and Hakibbutz Hameuchad.

———. 2016. "From Ethiopia to Israel: Migration and Ritual Roles of Beta Israel Women." *Clio, Women, Gender, History* 44 (2): 155–68.

Appadurai, Arjun. 1998. "Dead Certainty: Ethnic Violence in the Era of Globalization." *Development and Change* 29 (4): 905–25.

Appleyard, David. 2010. "Ethiopian Christianity." In *The Blackwell Companion to Eastern Christianity*, edited by Kenneth Parry, 117–36. Oxford: Wiley-Blackwell.

Artinian-Kaiser, Becky, David Clough, and Celia Deane-Drummond, eds. 2013. "The Study of Religion after the Animal." In *Animals as Religious Subjects: Transdisciplinary Perspectives*, 59–78. London: Bloomsbury.

Bakker, Egbert J. 2013. *The Meaning of Meat and the Structure of the Odyssey*. Cambridge: Cambridge University Press.

Baravelli, Giulio Cesare. 1935. *The Last Stronghold of Slavery: What Abyssinia Is*. Rome: Societa Editrice novissima.

Barthes, Roland. 1972. "Steak and Chips." In *Mythologies*, translated by Annette Lavers, 62–64. New York: Hill and Wang.

Bauer, Dan Franz. 1977. *Household and Society in Ethiopia: An Economic and Social Analysis of Tigray Social Principles and Household Organization*. East Lansing: Michigan State University Press.

Beidelman, Thomas O. 1966. "The Ox and Nuer Sacrifice: Some Freudian Hypotheses about Nuer Symbolism." *Man (New Series)* 1 (4): 453–67.

Ben Dor, Shoshana. 1985. "Ha'sigd Shel Beta Israel: Hag Hidush Ha'brith" [The Sigd of Beta Israel]. MA thesis, Hebrew University of Jerusalem.

———. 1987a. "The Journey towards Eretz Israel: the Story of Abba Mahari." [In Hebrew.] *Pe'amim* 33:5–32.

———. 1987b. "The Sigd of Beta Israel: Testimony to a Community in Transition." In *Ethiopian Jews and Israel*, edited by Michael Ashkenazi and Alex Weingrod, 140–59. New Brunswick, NJ: Transaction Publishers.

Ben-Ezer, Gadi. 2002. *The Ethiopian Jewish Exodus: Narratives of the Migration Journey to Israel, 1977–1985*. London: Routledge.

Biale, David, ed. 2002. *Cultures of the Jews: A New History*. New York: Schocken Books.

———. 2007. *Blood and Belief: The Circulation of a Symbol between Jews and Christians*. Berkeley: University of California Press.

Bohannan, Paul, and George Dalton, eds. 1962. "The Abyssinian Market Town." In *Markets in Africa*, 386–408. Evanston, IL: Northwestern University Press.

Boyarin, Daniel. 1995. *Carnal Israel: Reading Sex in Talmudic Culture*. Berkeley: University of California Press.

Boylston, Tom. 2012. "The Shade of the Divine: Approaching the Sacred in an Ethiopian Orthodox Christian Community." PhD diss., London School of Economics and Political Science (LSE).

———. 2013. "Food, Life and Material Religion in Ethiopian Orthodox Christianity." In *A Companion to the Anthropology of Religion*, edited by Janice Boddy and Michael Lambeck, 257–73. London: Wiley-Blackwell.

Bruce, James. 1790. *Travels to Discover the Source of the Nile, in the Years 1768, 1769, 1770, 1771, 1772, and 1773: In Five Volumes*. Edited by C. F. Beckingham. Edinburgh: Edinburgh University Press.

Buscemi, Francesco. 2018. *From Body Fuel to Universal Poison: Cultural History of Meat: 1900–The Present*. Cham, Switzerland: Springer International.

Cahoone, Lawrence. 2009. "Hunting as a Moral Good." *Environmental Values* 18 (1): 67–88.

Calame-Griaule, Geneviève, and Ziedonis Ligers. 1961. "L'Homme-hyène dans la tradition soudanaise." *L'Homme* 1 (2): 89–118.

Carter, Jeffrey, ed. 2003. *Understanding Religious Sacrifice: A Reader*. London: Continuum.

———. 2003. "General Introduction." In *Understanding Religious Sacrifice: A Reader*, edited by Jeffrey Carter, 1–11. London: Continuum.

Chaillot, Christine. 2002. *The Ethiopian Orthodox Tewahedo Church Tradition: A Brief Introduction to Its Life and Spirituality*. Paris: Inter-Orthodox Dialogue.

Cicurel, Inbal and Rachel Sharaby. 2007. "Women in the Menstruation Huts: Variations in Preserving Purification Customs among Ethiopian Immigrants." *Journal of Feminist Studies in Religion* 23 (2): 69–84.

Cofman-Simhon, Sarit. 2013. "African Tongues on the Israeli Stage: A Reversed Diaspora." *The Drama Review* 57 (3): 48–68.

Comaroff, Jean, and John L. Comaroff. 1990. "Goodly Beasts, Beastly Goods: Cattle and Commodities in a South African Context." *American Ethnologist* 17 (2): 195–216.

Corinaldi, Michael. 1998. *Jewish Identity: The Case of Ethiopian Jewry*. Jerusalem: Magnes Press, Hebrew University.

Crummey, Donald. 1980. "Abyssinian Feudalism." *Past & Present* 89 (1): 115–38.

———. 2000. *Land and Society in the Christian Kingdom of Ethiopia: From the Thirteenth to the Twentieth Century.* Champaign, IL: University of Illinois Press.

Deane-Drummond, Celia, and David Clough, eds. 2009. *Creaturely Theology: On God, Humans and Other Animals.* London: SCM.

Deane-Drummond, Celia, David Clough, and Rebecca Artinian-Kaiser, eds. 2013. "Introduction." In *Animals as Religious Subjects: Transdisciplinary Perspectives.* London: Bloomsbury T&T Clark.

Derrick, Jonathan. 1975. *Africa's Slaves Today.* New York: Schocken Books.

Djerrahian, Gabriella. 2018. "The 'End of Diaspora' Is Just the Beginning: Music at the Crossroads of Jewish, African, and Ethiopian Diasporas in Israel." *African and Black Diaspora: An International Journal* 11 (2): 161–73.

Doleve-Gandelman, Tsili. 1990. "Ethiopia as a Lost Imaginary Space: The Role of Ethiopian Jewish Women in Producing the Ethnic Identity of Their Immigrant Group in Israel." In *The Other Perspective in Gender and Culture: Rewriting Women and the Symbolic,* edited by Juliet Flower MacCannell, 242–57. New York: Columbia University Press.

Donham, Donald. 1986. "Old Abyssinia and the New Ethiopian Empire: Themes in Social History." In *The Southern Marches of Imperial Ethiopia: Essays in History and Social Anthropology,* edited by Donald Donham and Wendy James, 3–48. Cambridge: Cambridge University Press.

Dorson, Richard Mercer. 1972. "Africa and the Folklorist." In *African Folklore,* 3–67. Bloomington: Indiana University Press.

Douglas, Mary. 1966. *Purity and Danger: An Analysis of Concepts of Pollution and Taboo.* London: Routledge & Kegan Paul.

———. 1972. "Deciphering a Meal." *Daedalus: Myth, Symbol, and Culture* 101 (1): 61–81.

———. 2008. *Natural Symbols: Explorations in Cosmology.* London: Routledge.

Dubosson, Jérôme. 2014. "Human Self and Animal Other: The Favorite Animal among the Hamar." In *Ethiopian Images of Self and Other* (Schriften des Zentrums für Interdisziplinäre Regionalstudien 2), edited by Felix Girke, 83–104. Halle, Ger.: Universitätsverlag Halle-Wittenberg.

Dundes, Alan. 1981. "Wet and Dry, the Evil Eye: An Essay in Indo-European and Semitic Worldview." In *The Evil Eye: A Folklore Casebook,* 257–312. New York: Garland.

———. 1989. "The Ritual Murder or Blood Libel Legend: A Study of Anti-Semitic Victimization through Projective Inversion." *Temenos* 25:7–32.

Evangelatou, Maria. 2013. "The Symbolic Language of Ethiopian Crosses: Visualizing History, Identity and Salvation Through Form and Ritual." 2013 Hawaii University International Conferences: Art, Humanities, and Social Sciences.

Evans-Pritchard, Edward Evan. 1940. *The Nuer: A Description of the Modes of Livelihood and Political Institutions of a Nilotic People.* Oxford: Oxford University Press.

Fajans, Jane. 1988. "The Transformative Value of Food: A Review Essay." *Food and Foodways* 3 (1–2): 143–66.

Feeley-Harnik, Gillian. 1981. *The Lord's Table: Eucharist and Passover in Early Christianity.* Philadelphia: University of Pennsylvania Press.

———. 1995. "Religion and Food: An Anthropological Perspective 1." *Journal of the American Academy of Religion* 63 (3): 565–82.

Fenster, Tovi. 1998. "Ethnicity, Citizenship, Planning and Gender: The Case of Ethiopian Immigrant Women in Israel." *Gender, Place and Culture* 5 (2): 177–89.

Fernyhough, Timothy Derek. 2002. "Women, Gender History, and Slavery in Nineteenth-Century Ethiopia." Fourth Avignon Conference on Slavery and Forced Labour in Honour of Suzanne Miers: University of Avignon.

———. 2010. *Serfs, Slaves, and Shifta: Modes of Production and Resistance in Pre-Revolutionary Ethiopia.* Addis Ababa: Shama Books.

Fiddes, Nick. 1991. *Meat: A Natural Symbol.* London: Routledge.

Ficquet, Eloi. 2006. "Flesh Soaked Faith: Meat as a Marker of the Boundary between Christians and Muslims in Ethiopia." In *Muslim-Christian Encounters in Africa*, edited by Benjamin F. Soares, 39–56. Leiden: Brill.

Firth, Raymond. 1963. "Offering and Sacrifice: Problems of Organization." *The Journal of the Royal Anthropological Institute of Great Britain and Ireland* 93 (1): 12–24.

Flad, Johann Martin. 1869. *The Falashas of Abysinnia.* London: William Macintosh.

Friedman, Menahem. 1972. "The Chief Rabbinate: Dilemma without Solution." [In Hebrew.] *Medina U'Memshal* 3:118–22.

———. 1982. *Society and Religion: The Non-Zionist Orthodoxy in Eretz-Israel, 1918–1936.* [In Hebrew.] Jerusalem: Yad Ben-Zvi.

Garine, Igor de. 2005. "The Trouble with Meat: An Ambiguous Food." *Estudio del Hombre* 19:33–54.

Geertz, Clifford. 1974. "'From the Native's Point of View': On the Nature of Anthropological Understanding." *Bulletin of the American Academy of Arts and Sciences* 28 (1): 26–45.

Gelaye, Getie. 1999. "Contemporary Amharic Oral Poetry from Gojjam: Classification and a Sample Analysis." *Aethiopica: International Journal of Ethiopian and Eritrean Studies* 2:124–43.

Gennep, Arnold Van. 1960. *The Rites of Passage.* London: Routledge & Kegan Paul.

Gertz, Nurit, and Deborah Dash Moore. 2016. "What is Jewish Culture? Judaism as a Culture." *Jerusalem Post*, June 2016.

Goldberg, Harvey E., ed. 2001. *The Life of Judaism*. Berkeley: University of California Press.

———. 2018. "Anthropology and Hebrew Bible Studies: Modes of Interchange and Interpretation." *Brill Research Perspectives in Biblical Interpretation* 3 (1): 1–81.

Greenfield, Patricia, Oshrat Sulika Rotem, and Michael Weinstok. 2019. "Ethiopian Immigrants to Israel: The Persistence and Transformation of African Values and Practices in Art and Life." *Journal of Psychology in Africa* 29 (6): 613–24.

Griaule, Marcel. 1934. "L'esclavage en Abyssinie." *Etudes de Sociologie et d'Ethnologie Juridiques* 21 (May): 23–43.

Gromyko, A. A., ed. n.d. "Hierarchy at the Feast: The Partition of the Ox in Traditional Ethiopia." In *Proceedings of the Ninth International Congress of Ethiopian Studies, Moscow, 1988*, 3:173–92. Moscow: Nauka Publishers.

Gross, Aaron. 2014. *The Question of the Animal and Religion; Theoretical Stakes, Practical Implications*. New York: Columbia University Press.

Guindeuil, Thomas. 2014. "What do Christians (Not) Eat: Food Taboos and the Ethiopian Christian Communities (13th–18th c.)." *Annales d'Ethiopie* 29 (1): 59–82.

Gunchel, Ya 'akov. 2006. "Tezaze Sanbat." [In Hebrew.] *Eretz Acheret* 35:70–74.

———. 2008. "At the Breaking Point." [In Hebrew.] *Eretz Acheret* 44:24–27.

Halévy, Joseph. 1877. "Halévy's Travels in Abyssinia." In *Miscellany of Hebrew Literature*, 5–80. London: Wertheimer, Lea.

Haraway, Donna J. 2003. *The Companion Species Manifesto: Dogs, People, and Significant Otherness*. Chicago: University of Chicago Press.

Harris, Marvin. 1987. *The Sacred Cow and the Abominable Pig: Riddles of Food and Culture*. New York: Simon & Schuster.

Hastings, James. 1924. *Encyclopaedia of Religion and Ethics*. Edinburgh: T&T Clark.

Hendrickson, W. A., and K. B. Ward. 1975. "Atomic Models for the Polypeptide Backbones of Myohemerythrin and Hemerythrin." *Biochemical and Biophysical Research Communications* 66 (4): 1349–56.

Herbert, Eugenia W. 1993. *Iron, Gender and Power: Rituals of Transformation in African Societies*. Bloomington: Indiana University Press.

Herman, Marilyn. 2012. *Gondar's Child: Songs, Honor, and Identity among Ethiopian Jews in Israel*. Trenton, NJ: Red Sea.

Herskovits, Melville J. 1926a. "The Cattle Complex in East Africa." *American Anthropologist* 28 (1): 230–72.

———. 1926b. "The Cattle Complex in East Africa." *American Anthropologist* 28 (3): 494–528.

Hess, Robert. 1969. "Toward a History of the Falasha." In *Eastern African History*, edited by Daniel F. McCall, 107–32. New York: Frederick A. Praeger.

Hoben, Allan. 1970. "Social Stratification in Traditional Amhara Society." In *Social Stratification in Africa*, edited by Arthur Tuden and Leonard Plotnicov, 187–224. New York: Free Press Collier-Macmillan.

———. 1973. *Land Tenure among the Amhara of Ethiopia: The Dynamics of Cognatic Descent*. Chicago: University of Chicago Press.

Hoffman, Lawrence A. 1996. *Covenant of Blood: Circumcision and Gender in Rabbinic Judaism*. Chicago: University of Chicago Press.

Honea, Kenneth. 1956. "Buda in Ethiopia." *Wiener Volkerkundliche Mitteilungen* 4 (1): 20–24.

Hoskins, Janet. 2004. "Slaves, Brides and Other 'Gifts': Resistance, Marriage and Rank in Eastern Indonesia." *Slavery & Abolition* 25 (2): 90–107.

Hutchinson, Sharon. 1992. "The Cattle of Money and the Cattle of Girls among the Nuer, 1930–83." *American Ethnologist* 19 (2): 294–316.

———. 1996. *Nuer Dilemmas: Coping with Money, War, and the State*. Berkeley: University of California Press.

Isaac, Ephraim. 1995. "The Significance of Food in Hebraic-African Thought and the Role of Fasting in the Ethiopian Church." In *Asceticism*, edited by Vincent L. Wimbush and Richard Valantasis, 329–42. Oxford: Oxford University Press.

———. 2012. *The Ethiopian Orthodox Täwahïdo Church*. Trenton, NJ: Red Sea Press.

Jacoby, Karl. 1994. "Slaves by Nature? Domestic Animals and Human Slaves." *Slavery & Abolition* 15 (1): 89–99.

Jirata, Tadesse Jaleta. 2012. "Learning Through Play: An Ethnographic Study of Children's Riddling in Ethiopia." *Africa* 82 (2): 272–86.

———. 2017. "Oral Poetry as Herding Tool: A Study of Cattle Songs as Children's Art and Cultural Exercise among the Guji-Oromo in Ethiopia." *Journal of African Cultural Studies* 29 (3): 292–310.

Kaplan, Steven. 1987. "The Beta Israel (Falasha) Encounter with Protestant Missionaries: 1860–1905." *Jewish Social Studies* 49 (1): 27–42.

———. 1988. "The Beta Israel and the Rabbinate: Law, Ritual and Politics." *Social Science Information* 27 (3): 357–70.

———. 1990. *Les Falashas*. Turnhout, Belgium: Brepols.

———. 1992. *Beta Israel in Ethiopia: From Earliest Times to the Twentieth Century*. New York: New York University Press.

———. 1993. "Falasha Christians: A Brief History." *Midstream* 39 (1): 20–21.

———. 1999. "Everyday Resistance and the Study of Ethiopian Jews." In *The Beta Israel in Ethiopia and Israel: Studies on the Ethiopian Jews*, edited by Tudor Parfitt and Emanuela Trevisan-Semi, 113–27. London: Curzon.

Kaplan, Steven, and Chaim Rosen. 1993. "Ethiopian Immigrants in Israel: Between Preservation of Culture and Invention of Tradition." *The Jewish Journal of Sociology* 35 (1): 35–48.

———. 1994. "Ethiopian Jews in Israel." In *American Jewish Yearbook 1994*, edited by D. Singer and R. Seldin. Vol. 94. New York: American Jewish Committee.

———. 1996. "Created in Their Own Image: A Comment on Beta Israel Figurines." *Cahiers d'Etudes Africaines* 36 (141–142): 171–82.

Kaplan, Steven, and Hagar Salamon. 2004. "Ethiopian Jews in Israel: A Part of the People or Apart from the People?" In *Jews in Israel: Contemporary Social and Cultural Patterns*, edited by Uzi Rebhun and Chaim Isaac Waxman. Hanover, NH: Brandeis University Press.

Karadawi, Ahmed. 1991. "The Smuggling of the Ethiopian Falasha to Israel through Sudan." *African Affairs* 90 (358): 23–50.

Kessler, David. 1985. *The Falashas: The Forgotten Jews of Ethiopia*. New York: Schocken Books.

Kifleyesus, Abbebe. 2003. "Food." In *Encyclopaedia Aethiopica*, edited by Siegbert Uhlig, 2:560–65. Wiesbaden: Harrasowitz.

Kirshenblatt, Mayer, and Barbara Kirshenblatt-Gimblett. 2007. *They Called Me Mayer July: Painted Memories of a Jewish Childhood in Poland before the Holocaust*. Berkeley: University of California Press.

Korabiewicz, Waclaw. 1973. *The Ethiopian Cross*. Addis Ababa: Holy Trinity Cathedral.

Kraemer, David Charles. 2008. *Jewish Eating and Identity Through the Ages*. Routledge Advances in Sociology 29. London: Routledge.

Krempel, Veronika. 1972. *Die Soziale Und Wirtschaftliche Stellung Der Falascha in Der Christlich-Amharischen Gesellschaft von Nordwest-Äthiopien*. Berlin: Im Selbstverlag.

———. 1974. "Eine Berufskaste in Nordwest-Äthiopien—die Kayla (Falascha)." *Sociologus* 24 (1): 37–55.

Kristeva, Julia. 1982. *Powers of Horror: An Essay on Abjection*. Translated by Leon S. Roudiez. New York: Columbia University Press.

Larebo, Haile Mariam. 1988. "The Ethiopian Orthodox Church." In *Eastern Christianity and Politics in the Twentieth Century*, edited by Pedro Ramet, 375–99. Durham, NC: Duke University Press.

Leitman, Eva M. 1993. "Ethiopian Immigrant Women: Transition to a New Israeli Identity." PhD diss., Ohio State University.

Leroy, Paul E. 1979. "Slavery in the Horn of Africa." *Horn of Africa* 2 (3): 10–19.

Leslau, Wolf. 1946. "A Falasha Religious Dispute." *Proceedings of the American Academy for Jewish Research* 16:71–95.

———. 1951. *Falasha Anthology*. Yale Judaica Series 6. New Haven, CT: Yale University Press.

———. 1976. *Concise Amharic Dictionary: Amharic-English, English-Amharic*. Wiesbaden: Otto Harrassowitz.

Levine, Donald N. 1965. *Wax and Gold Tradition and Innovation in Ethiopian Culture*. Vol. 11. Chicago: University of Chicago Press.

———. 1974. *Greater Ethiopia: The Evolution of a Multiethnic Society*. Chicago: University of Chicago Press.

Lévi-Strauss, Claude. 1969 (1964). *The Raw and the Cooked*. Translated by John Weightman and Doreen Weightman. London: Jonathan Cape.

Lewis, Herbert S. 1974. "Neighbors, Friends, and Kinsmen: Principles of Social Organization Among the Cushitic-Speaking Peoples of Ethiopia." *Ethnology* 13 (2): 145–57.

Lienhardt, Godfrey. 1961. *Divinity and Experience: The Religion of the Dinka*. Oxford: Oxford University Press.

Lifchitz, Deborah. 1939. "Un Sacrifice Chez Les Falachas, Juifs d'Abyssinie." *La Terre et La Vie* 9:116–23.

Lotan, Shai. 2009. "The Qesotch vs. the Rabbinate and the Municipality: Let Us Slaughter." [In Hebrew.] *Mekomon Netanya*, October 1, 2009.

Lovejoy, Paul E., and Jan S. Hogendorn. 1993. *Slow Death for Slavery: The Course of Abolition in Northern Nigeria 1897–1936*. Cambridge: Cambridge University Press.

"Masa Be-'ikvot Ha-Basar." [In Hebrew.] 2009. Beta Israel: Society and Culture - Jews of Ethiopia. July 10. www.beteisrael.co.il/article.asp?ArtId =502&cat=חדשות, accessed January 2010.

Mauss, Marcel. 1966. *The Gift: Forms and Functions of Exchange in Archaic Societies*. London: Cohen & West.

McCann, James. 1988. "'Children of the House': Slavery and Its Suppression in Lasta, Northern Ethiopia, 1916–1935." In *The End of Slavery in Africa*, edited by Suzanne Miers and Richard L. Roberts, 332–61. Madison: University of Wisconsin Press.

———. 1995. *People of the Plow: An Agricultural History of Ethiopia 1800–1990*. Madison: University of Wisconsin Press.

Melamed, Abraham. 2003. *The Image of the Black in Jewish Culture: A History of the Other*. London: Routledge-Curzon.

Mendelson-Maoz, Adia. 2013. "Diaspora and Homeland—Israel and Africa in Beta Israel's Hebrew Literature and Culture." *Research in African Literatures* 44 (4): 35–50.

Messing, Simon David. 1957. "The Highland-Plateau of Ethiopia." PhD diss., University of Pennsylvania.

———. 1962. "The Abyssinian Market Town." In *Markets in Africa*, edited by Paul Bohannan and George Dalton, 386–408. Evanston, IL: Northwestern University Press.

———. 1975. "Health Care, Ethnic Outcasting, and the Problem of Overcoming the Syndrome of Encapsulation in a Peasant Society." *Human Organization* 34 (4): 395–97.

Miers, Suzanne. 2003. "Slavery: A Question of Definition." *Slavery and Abolition* 24 (2): 1–16.

Mintz, Sidney W., and Christine M. Du Bois. 2002. "The Anthropology of Food and Eating." *Annual Review of Anthropology* 31 (1): 99–119.

Morrison, Toni. 1987. *Beloved.* New York: Plume.

Nahon, Shmuel. 2006. "Shhita lefi ha-masoret ha-etiopit [Ritual slaughter according to Ethiopian tradition]." [In Hebrew.] *Kol Ha-Sharon*, April 8, 2006.

Narayan, Kirin. 2012. *Alive in the Writing: Creating Ethnography in the Company of Chekhov.* Chicago: University of Chicago Press.

Nicolas, Andrea. 2006. "Governance, Ritual and Law: Tulama-Oromo Gadaa Assemblies." In *Proceedings of the 15th International Conference of Ethiopian Studies Hamburg, 2003,* edited by Uhlig Siegberg, 168–76. Wiesbaden: Harrassowitz.

Nietzche, Friedrich Wilhelm. 1981. *The Use and Abuse of History.* Translated by Adrian Collins. Indianapolis: Bobbs-Merrill Educational Publishing.

Ortner, Sherry B. 1973. "On Key Symbols." *American Anthropologist* 75 (5): 1338–46.

Pankhurst, Richard. 1976. "The History of the Bareya, Sanqella and Other Ethiopian Slaves from the Borderlands of the Sudan." *Sudan Notes and Records* 58:1–43.

———. 1988. "Hierarchy at the Feast: The Partition of the Ox in Traditional Ethiopia." In *Proceedings of the Ninth International Congress of Ethiopian Studies,* Vol. 3, edited by A. A. Gromyko, 173–92. Moscow: Nauka.

———. 1990. *A Social History of Ethiopia.* Addis Ababa: Institute of Ethiopian Studies, Addis Ababa University.

Parfitt, Tudor. 1985. *Operation Moses.* London: Weidenfeld and Nicolson.

Patai, Raphael. 1986. *The Seed of Abraham: Jews and Arabs in Contact and Conflict.* Salt Lake City: University of Utah Press.

Poluha, Eva, ed. 2007. "Growing Up in Town and in the Countryside in Amharic Society." In *The World of Girls and Boys in Rural and Urban Ethiopia,* 67–92. Addis Ababa: Forum for Social Studies.

Quirin, James Arthur. 1977. "The Beta Israel (Falasha) in Ethiopian History: Caste Formation and Culture Change, 1270–1868." PhD diss., University of Minnesota.

———. 1992. *The Evolution of the Ethiopian Jews: A History of the Beta Israel (Falasha) to 1920.* Philadelphia: University of Pennsylvania Press.

Rapoport, Louis. 1980. *The Lost Jews: Last of the Ethiopian Falashas.* New York: Stein and Day.

———. 1986. *Redemption Song: The Story of Operation Moses.* New York: Harcourt Brace Jovanovich.

Ratner, David. 2018. "Rap, Racism, and Visibility: Black Music as a Mediator of Young Israeli-Ethiopians' Experience of Being 'Black' in a 'White' Society." *African and Black Diaspora: An International Journal* 12 (1): 1–15.

Reed, Annette Yoshiko. 2013. "From Sacrifice to the Slaughterhouse: Ancient and Modern Approaches to Meat, Animals, and Civilization." *Method and Theory in the Study of Religion.* https://doi.org/10.1163/15700682-12341269.

Reminick, Ronald A. 1974. "The Evil Eye Belief among the Amhara of Ethiopia." *Ethnology* 13 (3): 279–91.

Rosen, Chaim. 1985. "Core Symbols of Ethiopian Identity and their Role in Understanding the Beta Israel Today." *Israel Social Science Research* 3 (1–2): 55–62.

———. 1987. "Hashaveh v'hashoneh ben Beta Yisrael beGondar v'beTigre [Similarities and differences between the Beta Israel of Gondar and Tigre]." [In Hebrew.] *Pe'amim* 33:93–108.

Sabar, Galia. 2020. "Re-thinking the Study of Religion: Lessons from Field Studies of Religions in Africa and the African Diaspora." In *Faith in African Lived Christianity,* edited by Karen Lauterbac and Mika Vähäkangas, 80–108. Leiden: Brill.

Sahlins, Marshall David. 1976. "La Pensée Bourgeoise: Western Society as Culture." In *Culture and Practical Reason.* Chicago: University of Chicago Press.

Salamon, Hagar. 1994a. "Between Ethnicity and Religiosity: Internal Group Aspects of Conversion among the Beta Israel in Ethiopia." [In Hebrew.] *Pe'amim* 58:104–19.

———. 1994b. "Slavery among the 'Beta-Israel' in Ethiopia: Religious Dimensions of Inter-Group Perceptions." *Slavery & Abolition* 15 (1): 72–88.

———. 1995. "Metaphors as Corrective Exegesis: Three Proverbs of the Beta-Israel." *Proverbium* 12:295–313.

———. 1999. *The Hyena People: Ethiopian Jews in Christian Ethiopia.* Berkeley: University of California Press.

———. 2001. "In Search of Self and Other: A Few Remarks on Ethnicity, Race, and Ethiopian Jews." In *Jewish Locations: Traversing Racialized Landscapes,* edited by Lisa Tessman and Bat-Ami Bar On. Lanham, MD: Rowan & Littlefield.

———. 2002. "Between Conscious and Subconscious: Depth-to-Depth Communication in the Ethnographic Space." *Ethos* 30 (3): 249–72.

———. 2003. "Blackness in Transition: Decoding Racial Constructs through Stories of Ethiopian Jews." *Journal of Folklore Research* 40 (1): 3–32.

———. 2008a. "Bein Amharim ve'Tigrinim: Narrative Shel Pitsul Ba Maavar meEtiopia leIsrael" [In between Amhara and Tigray people: Narrating a split in the passage from Ethiopia to Israel]. Conference on Ethiopian Jews: The Open University, Ra'anana, Israel.

———. 2008b. "Cow Tales: Decoding Images of Slavery in the Ethiopian Jewish Community." *Slavery & Abolition* 29 (3): 415–35.

———. 2010. "Misplaced Home and Mislaid Meat: Stories Circulating among Ethiopian Immigrants in Israel." *Callaloo* 33 (1): 165–76.

———. 2011. "The Floor Falling Away: Dislocated Space and Body in the Humour of Ethiopian Immigrants in Israel." *Folklore* 122 (1): 16–34.

———. 2014. "Holy Meat, Black Slaughter: Power, Religion, Kosher Meat, and the Ethiopian-Israeli Community." In *Political Meals*, edited by Regina F. Bendix and Michaela Fenske, 273–85. Munster: Wissenchaftsforum Kulinaristik, LIT.

———. 2015. "Cutting into the Flesh of the Community: Ritual Slaughter, Meat Consumption, and the Transition from Ethiopia to Israel." *Studies in Contemporary Jewry* 28:110–45.

———. 2017a. "Meat Lottery: A Spectacle in Transition from Ethiopia to Israel." *African and Black Diaspora* 11 (2): 129–43.

———. 2017b. "Spices for Thought: Salt, Chili-Pepper and Slaves in Ethiopian Amharic Proverbs." *Northeast African Studies* 17 (2): 101–30.

———. 2019. "From Hand to Mouth: Reflections on the Multi-Vocality of Gursha in Ethiopia." *Northeast African Studies* 19 (2): 1–30.

Salamon, Hagar and Harvey Goldberg. 2016. "Muslims in the Synagogue." [In Hebrew.] *The New East: Journal of the Middle East and Islamic Studies* 55:61–84.

Salamon, Hagar, Steven Kaplan, and Harvey Goldberg. 2009. "What Goes Around, Comes Around: Rotating Credit Associations among Ethiopian Women in Israel." *African Identities* 7 (3): 399–415.

Sanbatu, Iyanho Farade. 2005. "The Way to Religious Independence Goes through Separate Slaughter." *Ha'aretz*, November 17, 2005.

Sawyer, Roger. 1986. *Slavery in the Twentieth Century*. London: Routledge & Kegan Paul.

Schneider, David Murray, Janet L. Dolgin, David S. Kemnitzer, and Victor Turner, eds. 1977. "Symbols in African Rituals." In *Symbolic Anthropology: A Reader in the Study of Symbols and Meanings*, 183–94. New York: Columbia University Press.

Schorsch, Jonathan. 2018. *The Food Movement, Culture, and Religion: A Tale of Pigs, Christians, Jews, and Politics*. Cham, Switzerland: Springer International.

Schwarz, Tanya. 2001. *Ethiopian Jewish Immigrants: The Homeland Postponed*. Richmond: Curzon Press.

Scott, James C. 1985. *Weapons of the Weak: Everyday Forms of Peasant Resistance*. New Haven, CT: Yale University Press.

———. 1990. *Domination and the Arts of Resistance: Hidden Transcripts*. New Haven, CT: Yale University Press.

Seeman, Don. 2003. "Agency, Bureaucracy, and Religious Conversion: Ethiopian 'Felashmura' Immigrants to Israel." In *The Anthropology of Religious Conversion*, edited by Andrew Buckser and Stephen D. Glazier, 29–42. Lanham, MD: Rowman & Littlefield.

———. 2009. *One People, One Blood: Ethiopian-Israelis and the Return to Judaism*. New Brunswick, NJ: Rutgers University Press.

———. 2015. "Coffee and the Moral Order: Ethiopian Jews and Pentecostals against Culture." *American Ethnologist* 42 (4): 734–48.

Seifu, Metaferia Ferewe. 1972. "Terminology for a 'Servant' (Slave?) in Amharic Tradition." *Journal of Ethiopian Studies* 10 (2): 127–200.

Seleshe, Semeneh, Cheorun Jo, and Mooha Lee. 2014. "Meat Consumption Culture in Ethiopia." *Korean Journal for Food Science of Animal Resources* 34 (1): 7–13.

Shabtay, Malka. 2003. "'Ragap': Music and Identity among Young Ethiopians in Israel." *Critical Arts* 17 (1–2): 93–105. https://doi.org/10.1080/025602403853100071.

———. 2006. *Yehudei Etiopia mi-zera Beta Israel: masa'am mi-"Beta Israel" le-bnei ha "Falashmura" ve-le-yehudei Etiopia.* [In Hebrew.] Tel Aviv: Lashon Tsecha.

Shabtay, Malka, and L. Kacen. 2005. *Mulualem: Ethiopian Women and Girls in Spaces, Worlds and Journeys Between Cultures.* [In Hebrew.] Tel Aviv: Lashon Tseha.

Shain, Yossi. 2019. *The Israeli Century and the Israelization of Judaism.* [In Hebrew.] Tel Aviv: Yediot Sfarim.

Shalom, Sharon. 2016. *From Sinai to Ethiopia.* Jerusalem: Gefen.

Shelemay, Kay Kaufman. 1986. *Music, Ritual, and Falasha History.* East Lansing: Michigan State University.

———. 1994. *A Song of Longing: An Ethiopian Journey.* Urbana-Champaign: University of Illinois Press.

Simoons, Frederick J. 1994. *Eat Not This Flesh: Food Avoidances from Prehistory to the Present.* 2nd ed. Madison: University of Wisconsin Press.

Spector, Stephen. 2005. *Operation Solomon: The Daring Rescue of the Ethiopian Jews.* Oxford: Oxford University Press.

Summerfield, Daniel. 2003. *From Falashas to Ethiopian Jews: The External Influences for Change c. 1860–1960.* London: Routledge Curzon.

Takla-Haymanot, Ayala. 1981. *The Ethiopian Church and Its Christological Doctrine.* Addis Ababa: Graphic Printers.

Talmi-Cohen, Ravit. 2014. "Aliyah as a Journey: The Four Stations of Zera Beita Israel (the Falashmura) between Ethiopia and Israel." [In Hebrew.] PhD diss., Tel Aviv University.

Tibebu, Teshale. 1995. *The Making of Modern Ethiopia: 1896–1974.* Trenton, NJ: Red Sea.

Trevisan-Semi, Emanuela. 1985. "The Beta Israel (Falashas): From Purity to Impurity." *Jewish Journal of Sociology* 27 (2): 103–14.

Turner, Victor. 1969. *The Ritual Process: Structure and Anti-Structure.* New York: Aldine.

Ullendorff, Edward. 1968. *Ethiopia and the Bible: The Schweich Lectures of the British Academy 1967.* London: British Academy and Oxford University Press.

Vas da Silva, Francisco. 2014. "Why Cinderella's Mother Becomes a Cow." *Marvels & Tales: Journal of Fairy-Tale Studies* 28 (1): 25–37.

Vialles, Noélie. 1994. *Animal to Edible*. Translated by J. A. Underwood. London: Cambridge University Press.

Wagner, Roy. 1986. *Symbols That Stand for Themselves*. Chicago: University of Chicago Press.

Waldman, Menahem. 1989. *Beyond the Rivers of Ethiopia: The Jews of Ethiopia and the Jewish People*. [In Hebrew.] Tel Aviv: Ministry of Defense.

———. 1991. *From Ethiopia to Jerusalem*. [In Hebrew.] Jerusalem: Ministry of Education and Culture.

Weber, Nicholas. 2005. "The Distribution and Use of Cattle Products in Northern Highland Ethiopia." MA thesis, Simon Fraser University.

Webster-Kogen, Ilana. 2016. "'Tezeta' (Nostalgia): Memory and Loss in Ethiopia and the Diaspora." In *Pieces of the Musical World: Sounds and Culture*, edited by Rachel Harris and Rowan Pease, 227–44. Abingdon, UK: Routledge.

———. 2018. *Citizen Azmari: Making Ethiopian Music in Tel Aviv*. Middletown, CT: Wesleyan University Press.

Weil, Shalva. 2004. "Ethiopian Jewish Women: Trends and Transformations in the Context of Transnational Change." *Nashim: A Journal of Jewish Women's Studies & Gender Issues* 8 (Fall): 73–86.

———. 2007. "Zionism and Aliya." [In Hebrew.] In *Ethiopia: Jewish Communities in the Nineteenth and Twentieth Centuries*, edited by Hagar Salamon, 187–200. Jerusalem: Ben-Zvi.

Wurmbrand, Max. 1971. "Falashas." In *Encyclopaedia Judaica*. Jerusalem: Keter.

Yerday, Efrat. 2021. "Who Narrates My Story?" [In Hebrew.] *Tikva Israelit*, Ben Gurion University. https://in.bgu.ac.il/cau/israeli-hope/pages/news/Ethiopian-Jews-storytelling.aspx.

Yuval, Israel Jacob. 2006. *Two Nations in Your Womb: Perceptions of Jews and Christians in Late Antiquity and the Middle Ages*. Berkeley: University of California Press.

Zellelew, Tilahun Bejitual. 2014. "Meat Abstinence and Its Positive Environmental Effect: Examining the Fasting Etiquettes of the Ethiopian Orthodox Church." *Critical Research on Religion* 2 (2): 134–46.

———. 2015a. "Religious Food Taboo as a Cause of Reciprocal Hospitality between Orthodox Christians and Muslims in Ethiopia." *Food Studies: An Interdisciplinary Journal* 5 (2): 1–11.

———. 2015b. "The Semiotics of the 'Christian/Muslim Knife': Meat and Knife as Markers of Religious Identity in Ethiopia." *Signs and Society* 3 (1): 44–70.

INDEX

Hagar Salamon is Max and Margarethe Grunwald Professor of Folklore and Folk Culture Studies and Senior Research Fellow at the Harry S. Truman Institute for the Advancement of Peace, both at the Hebrew University of Jerusalem. Her long-standing interest in cultural modes and practices in which issues of identity are conceived, negotiated, and renegotiated has inspired a wide range of studies. The Ethiopian Jews both in Ethiopia and in the State of Israel stand at their heart. Among her books are *The Hyena People: Ethiopian Jews in Christian Ethiopia* and *Israel in the Making: Stickers, Stitches, and Other Critical Practices.*